Pamphlet for Life

Spirit of Space with Gabriel et al. through Arthur Fanning

Other Publications by

Arthur Fanning

Soul Evolution Father

Simon

The Comprehension of the Holy Spirit within the Human Condition

Permission to Ascend

Pamphlet for Life

Spirit of Space with
Gabriel et al. through
Arthur Fanning

Light Technology Publishing

www.LightTechnology.com

For more information about special discounts for bulk purchases, please contact Light Technology Publishing Special Sales at 1-800-450-0985 or publishing@LightTechnology.net.

ISBN-13: 978-1-62233-040-9
Published and printed in the United States of America by

Light Technology Publishing

PO Box 3540
Flagstaff, AZ 86003
1-800-450-0985 • 928-526-1345
www.LightTechnology.com

This book is dedicated to the
benefit of the human condition.

Contents

Introduction

June 30, 2015

The planetary consciousness is shifting, and what you're witnessing in the expression is a recapitulation of everything that has happened before in your history and spiritual understandings raised to another level, where communication can take place at a different frequency. Down at this level, no one knew anything; now you're supposed to know something. This is part of the exposure. The cloak is coming off, and everything; there's nothing hidden. Yet within this process, discernment's required, a level of discernment that is not defined by the word "discernment." The word "discernment" gives you a clue that you must check your sources and be careful of what you choose. Yet the next level of discernment is your knowledge, which should already be there based on the truth of yourself. We'll stop there for the moment because this is what's going on in your world now.

This process that you're in (and by that, I mean world consciousness — world, not social, consciousness), social consciousness, is contained within the culture. America has social consciousness, Germany has social consciousness, England has social consciousness, and the Muslims have social consciousness — Syria, Iraq, and Iran. They each have a compartment of it. It's not the same. Intermixing in social consciousness are spiritual truths.

That's what social consciousness is based on, and so spiritual truths now are going to become evident out of necessity for the protection of the spiritual force within the human condition, within your self.

As you would say, you eat the proper food to stay healthy, so you contemplate proper thought to stay in a continuity of consciousness with your own spiritual development. You don't need to discuss reincarnation; you all know what that is there. You're finding yourselves in the stream of it now, and your abilities are going to be increased, yet you already know what they are because your spiritual force is going to go back to its beginning as a recognized self and come forward with the power only at this time, at another level of understanding.

Your clue to feeling better, number one, is nature, yeah, the planet itself, the space you're walking in, the air you're breathing, and the water you're drinking. That's all you really know. That's all you really know. The only consciousness you know within the self needs water. It needs, what you term, the magnetic and gravitational influences so that it can express in this density. It needs the breath of air and then the space to contemplate why, how, what you are, where, and when. Space is the grace given to you by what you understand is God, yet the space contains God everywhere between everything and everyone.

You beings like to say planes or dimensions, levels; they are really perceptive barriers, veils we will call them, because those are words that have been used, yet the awakening that is occurring within ones is you're going to see things differently. When the sight changes, or you're ability to see, what you call, within the psychic dimensional things, there is always a reaction to what has been seen. Usually it is a contemplative reaction to understand the seeing and then a defensive reaction to know whether you are safe or not. Then it's a participation reaction that you acknowledge you have been allowed to see and join.

Now, that joining phase, where you're joining in the participation of what the expression is you're seeing, is a cautionary phase, because once you've seen it, you are adjusted by it, number one. Yet you try to recall past experiences to validate and express self within these new concepts. You must let the new concepts introduce themselves to you because they are personalities who have presented themselves that allow you to see them. And it's a welcoming, yet in the condition of social consciousness, there is polite behavior and manners (and this, that). Yet you don't know the polite behavior and manners required in this new dimension.

You'll say dimension; it's not a dimension. You're already there. You just haven't allowed yourself to be expressed there. You have been, basically, intimidated into a position that is not yourself, and the intimidation comes from the, we're going to call it, religious fervor in the secular churches because the churches are separate. You have the Jewish tradition. You have the Muslim tradition. You have the Catholic tradition. You have the Baptist tradition. You have the Methodist tradition.

All of these little units are trying to explain the same concept here, moving in it, so when you get there, you are in a gentle space. Each one's trying to at least prepare, in a manner. That is what they were designed for, yet in your consciousness now, your churches have controlled you. They have shut off those abilities. They have been under the control of what has been referred to, and I will use that term, the master of discomfort. Those are the words people feel more comfortable with, I guess. That one has been — what you say? — messing with everyone on all levels, many levels, many, many levels. The discernment now is to recognize that, to recognize that. So as your mind, not the brain, goes back to its time of its first inception and knowledge of itself, it brings forth the power that is not confused by this other one.

So this is what's going on now, the awakening of humanity in everyone, and as it happens, the awakening, everyone defines their choices and sort of shows their accomplishments. They have succeeded in doing "this" and "this" and "this," and everyone's allowed "this" and "that," yet the spiritual teachings that allowed you to come forth in the first place have been disregarded, and now you're going to face the confusion of it all. That is what is going on.

The Invisible Is Manifesting through the Acknowledgment of Consciousness

The consciousness of the human condition has reached a level of pure panic, basically. The confirmation of this is going to be when the planet Nibiru becomes more visible in the consciousness of the human condition. Then you are going to meet the old ones — the old ones *before* the old ones, the old ones before Moses [laughs], before Abraham, those beings, *before*.

The warnings have been laid out long ago. You have had many things hidden from you that are going to come out. Right now, there is a letter written by Mohammed that has been found. It is available, and it tells the Muslims ... because Mohammed was — Jesus said Mohammed was coming. Mohammed came and brought another teaching or more teaching, actually. The Koran was given, which was written by Gabriel. That was the process, and as you understand these things, the letter from Mohammed was told for the Muslims to protect the Christians, to not make them do "this" and "that." They have their laws, and Muslims have their laws under the same divine entity that brought forth both Jesus and Mohammed.

It says to pay attention to that in this letter. Yet it is not happening. So the spiritual authority that was given to these prophets has been undermined. You're going through that process. What you're going to find out is that you are all spiritual prophets because you are going to understand the manifestation of your body with proper food, proper breathing, proper water, and proper thought.

The human condition is going to understand the importance of itself, not only in the fact that you can move and you can breathe, and you didn't know why you had to breathe. But you're going to understand the concept of air and the importance that you as an entity before being born have given to yourself and received for yourself. You are going to be aware that others in your environment are not aware of that, but you are going to feel the energy they should be.

Yet now this is where the word "humility" is needed to calm yourself down because you are going to have many beings claiming they are Christ. It's already started to happen — that they were Jesus and they are Jesus, and this. What you're feeling — what they're feeling — is the presence of the knowledge of the truth of it, basically. It's not them. It is the invisible manifesting through what, as you say, is the physical acknowledging that consciousness. Yet it is not them. They think it is. But it is a force that comes in to heal the body, and it frightens the ego because it's a truth as it is — because it is the truth that Jesus is Jesus and the message given.

Then the self understands its, well, it has a fear of its (how do you say?) false workings, we'll call it, because they are not Jesus, or they're not the Virgin Mary. Yet it is like a medium that poses frequencies. It's not them, and some get caught in it and the scythe, the sickle, of Saturn begins to take hold or have an effect.

Saturn has a frequency. It, Saturn, is prevalent now. It's what everyone is feeling — Saturn and the myth of eating his children and cutting the wings off Cupid and that thing, that sort of force of not recognizing other things, basically. It is a time thing with Saturn. That's why we say time is a direction, and you understand the direction is up. You essentially lift yourself up above the scythe, or the sickle, of Saturn. You move above it, and it doesn't get you, in a manner. And the "getting you" is the confusion of the ability of self to heal itself, the confusion of the self and its ability to heal itself, because you are caught in time, and time is an anchor.

Time is an anchor. It's an anchor. It anchors the self within space, and space is the Grace. The concept of no time should be the pleasant experience of the space until Saturn comes in to add density to you. That process is not understood yet.

When you move — we are going to have to say it this way — when you move through your Moon (and this is an expression that people have not heard before, but you do move through the Moon), and the (you call them) moon phases affect you, yes. But you are moving through the Moon, and you know it. It's like swimming. It's just swimming in a different emotional bond, basically. You have a different knowledge, eventually, of what breath it took to move through that phenomenon.

The only thing that moves you in the emotional context, really, is your breath. That's the importance of tantric breathing, so you can stay centered and stable within the condition of yourself. That is why it is important to understand which nostril you're breathing in and eventually for what reason, because the left nostril excites, what you call, the optical nerves within the left eye. The right nostril will excite the optical nerves in the right eye, which will cause the great generation, we will say, that occurs in the back of the brain that allows the seven eyes here to open. So you see many things at once. It will be like looking at an apartment building and seeing all the rooms open at the same time, like looking through glass, seeing everything in each room, and knowing the individual participants are not aware of the other rooms. But you will see all going on.

This opening is starting to occur, and the confusion is going to be when "this" happens, you need to be able to identify the master who taught you — you have to — and the feeling and understanding of it in a spiritual sense, what you would term angels, you can say. You can say proper thought experienced within the system of self and the realization of proper thought expressed and performed by you because there is always a performance in this world.

You Are Going to Be a Ball of Light

Eventually, you are going to learn to walk like the Buddhas, the monks — the beings that be in space all over the place. You have more than two arms. You have many arms. You have many appendages, and it's the unification of these things that causes you to understand your greater brilliance. Literally, your bones will go into a more crystalline energy frequency, and the light begins to be broadcast from the bones through the skin.

Eventually, you're going to have to understand that you are going to turn into a ball of light. Part of you will be here [out to the left]. That part will see the ball of light, and the ball of light is communicating, doing things. But the conscious physical form that you think you have, or your idea of yourself, will be here above it; you'll see it. Anyone participating with you as you go through this transition will just see the ball of light. They will think the ball of light is talking. Yet the fear of that transition, as you say, this one we did now, the ball that went to light, you have confusion, so as the transition begins for ones to go into a ball of light, the holographic memory of what the being looked like is held by you so that you don't confuse yourself talking to a ball of light. You think the image is there, yet it isn't. You think the person is there, yet the person isn't.

This is where people are going to fall down. Those balls of light that you see in the sky that people are taking pictures of during your day, they are not UFOs. I know they call them orbs, but they are beings of light. Then that one ball, or orb, can expand, and it'll be a person or an entity who comes out of it. Yet it knows it is going to be this ball; that is what it prefers right now. So you're going to go into that and join the balls of light. You are going to become balls of light. Yet that shifting back and forth creates the fear thing because you have not done it before. You're not aware of it yet, "Wait! Come back. What happened?"

Wait, shifting. You mean being physical, then a ball of light, and then being physical? How fast? Is it too fast for someone to see?

Well, no, you'll see it. You'll feel it, and then what will happen is fear will take over because it's never happened before. When you come back from being a ball of light into a physical form, you could just smack yourself right into a wall because you are not aware where the ball of light is moving. So you are going to have to be careful. Your arms are going to start disappearing; that's the first thing. The ankles are going to have pain because the ankles are the ones that keep you in the magnetic influence. Then you will have to train those forces there that it is okay to let go, in a manner.

This is the way you learn to have your posture. And the posture has been presented to you — the correct posture, by the way — in the images that you see of the beings sitting by the doorway of Egyptian temples. Those giant statues sitting there erect and staid hold the frequency for the continuity of consciousness because what you are really doing in your world, you are terming it ascension, but we have told you it is a descension. So you are holding force for the self to feel safe in this process of ascension and descension.

It's like you're going to bed and waking up in the morning. You don't know what occurs in the time you are sleeping; you presume you're safe because you woke up. So you're in the reconstructive process of the body with knowledge, permission, and assent, we'll call it, and that assent is like a secret word. You go up, and you get this secret gift. It is usually, what we would term, a gold envelope for you to understand it's a message. Then you bring it back, and it's opened within you but not in the conscious mind.

As the envelope is opened, the healing butterflies, we'll call them, the little entities that have been gifted to you, they automatically go and fix, because they know what they're doing, and adjust. The liver and kidneys now are taking a majority of the hits. So is the spleen. You need to be delicate with yourself in the human condition, now particularly.

When you are drinking your water, have thankfulness for the water. Now, you know that California's going through this drought thing, and that's big news, and no one still respects the water. They want it. The water is taking itself away. It's taking itself away because of the disrespect for it. That is what is happening. That's what's happening. The beings do not deserve the water, and the water knows. In your ancient books, it says God's path is through the water. Disrespect for the water is disrespect for the concept of God. It does not matter what religion you are in. It doesn't matter. Everyone needs water. So your attention is being drawn to the divine aspect of God to the water, literally. Literally.

You have beings now in the concepts of understanding for food;

they thank the earth for producing food. You should thank God for producing the seed that grew the food. The receptacle produces, but it is not what should be thanked. You thank the earth for being the earth but you thank the Divine for providing the ability and all the people who delivered food to your table, every one of them. You thank the seed first. But you have a confusion in consciousness now.

The Ancient Prayer Within You

There is a grand, defiant argument against God going on now. That is what the Supreme Court decision did. You've all heard of Sodom and Gomorrah, and you've all heard of Lot. "Don't turn right; don't turn back." This happened, and you're repeating it. It is being repeated, yet the repetition is not understood. There's an arrogance and ignorance there of seeming success. For what? Sexual gratification? Misinterpretation of the purpose of your life? And you're going to have to understand this because the suffering is going to be great. The process has started.

You have your July 2015 to go through. You have your July. We warned about this one. We have said you will be thankful for August. We told you the Lord's Prayer is for the Lords by the Lords to the Lords from the Lords. It is a collapse of the 150 psalms. It was too difficult for people to understand, so Jesus reduced it. You pause with what you say and have knowledge of what you are saying and ask for, yet it's not occurring. So the human condition now is going to be faced with their own choices.

Prayer is needed, the simplest one and the safest one, and for those with limited understanding in your desire for protection is Psalm 6 because it asks particularly in the tenth verse for your enemies to be ashamed — not to hurt them physically, but for the shame. It doesn't mean the physical entities, yet it applies. It means those spiritual forces above you that are mocking you and laughing at you because of your inadequacies of your ability to think for yourself in an appropriate manner. There are beings doing that. It's been throughout the churches.

Your religious leaders are finding themselves in great turmoil now in their own understanding because of, what you call, markers, markers. We will call them markers, pyramids. You're finding them on Mars now, same structure. Look for it. They are signal points, actually coordination pinpoints for energy forces from the nonexistent to become existent. Mars, the planet Mars, you term Mars, is the warrior planet. You know the energy of that planet. How was that manifested? It's from the first creations of the anger beings. The original one took that force that was being created by the ignorance and condensed it into this planetary system called Mars for a run around so that they could feel it later, not all at once — same thing with Venus, same thing with Jupiter, Saturn, Neptune. All of these forces for understanding confusion that you were manipulating, the being took it and made this little play ball for you here, okay. They want that, will put that "there" and put that "there," and put them in the middle. The light of the Sun is in the middle, and everything else goes around it.

The Creator, well, you will use that word "Creator," God, took the misappropriate — inappropriate — thoughts and constructed your planets for you, same thing with all these other systems, because life is, what you term, perpetual and should be forever for everything within the conditions set, the condition's set. You were born, and conditions were set. You were born with bones, flesh, skin, sinew, and overlays, yet within you, you know you're not the bone. You know you're not the flesh. You know you're not the skin. But when your skin is cut or your flesh is deepened with the penetration, you'll feel it; part of you feels it. It's a feeling sensation of you, yet the emotional sensation is not really understood in the appreciation of the God force that is you.

You are forming opinions based on others' words instead of the prayers of yourself. Every human being on your planet has an ancient prayer within. Babies babble it when they are doing just their little "la la." They are doing it. They know what it is. They are making connections deep in the cellular structures. If you have noticed, the consciousness of little ones who are coming up are more aware. The consciousness of the older generation is going to become more childish. This is what you call the Alzheimer's thing. That's the way it should be. Yet when you understand what Alzheimer's is, it is a punishment of the self for inappropriate behavior. You don't want to face what you have done, so you have to turn away.

Water Is Your Blessing

The most appropriate three words you can use now are "Father, have mercy." And inside, the deepness of your self knows what that means. When that is put there, then the nurturing aspect of the holy mother, you term the queen of heaven, comes to assure you that mercy will be given. She comes. She's the dark cloak. If you look in your stars at night, the blackness between the stars is her cloak, and those stars are on her robe. You are each a star on her robe somewhere. That is how she knows you.

So when you ask for the mercy from the Father, the divine influence (pick a name because you have issues with names), she allows the nurturing and protection because too much of the other force can obliterate everything. It turns everything to salt, pretty much. It wipes out all conditions of moisture. It just takes it right away completely because you don't respect it. It is what provides the ability for movement in life — water and air. The human condition is trying to learn the sanctity of the four elements. You realize the fifth element, which is a tree, to provide you the oxygen to breathe. So there's a consciousness being connected with nature and the appreciation of it.

The trees and water are going to be so important to you that you are not going to want to leave them, eventually, because you understand that even the tree, as it produces this availability of oxygen, also calls within itself demonic forces that would damage the human condition to transfer those forces into an expression that can be used to perpetuate life, and as that transition takes place within you in the human condition, the demonic forces are no longer demonic. They educate themselves through the tree and through the human. Some are now learning and understanding, what you say, exorcisms to place these beings into trees, the spirits that are influencing people to do negative things. As they go into trees, the spirits are relieved because the trees flow down the energy, yet it knows it's going to progress because it is going to be a breath eventually for someone. That is what it really wants because it is not physical.

Your connection with the trees has been forgotten, really. You are working toward that because your bones have a similar understanding of a tree, and the bones have a similar understanding of feathers and wings. The similar understanding is that you are all things. Soon the trees are going to talk to you, and the rocks are going to talk. There are beings in those rocks, yet they are not greater than you. You are with them for a reason.

Now, as you live your life, it is not death. Yet as you have lived your life, you're not thirteen anymore. You're not fourteen.

You're not fifteen. You're not twenty, and you're not forty. Those personalities have collapsed, yet the memories are there holding consciousness. They're developing a new personality that thanks those young ones who participated within the body of you to get you this far. Those personalities within the young ones are, what you say, going through the enjoyment. How is that? It is when you have a memory of your childhood. That young one is there bringing that memory back, wanting to be thanked. Whether it is a good experience or a bad experience, it participated in the experience, but you are here because of that experience, whatever it was.

So in the suffering of a child, that energy comes back, and you remember. You bless it and thank it because you went through it with this condition of an educated self. You worked with the process, as a little one, of understanding evil, recognizing it as it manifested toward you, literally. You learn how to avoid this now in other thought streams; that's the process. That is what is occurring.

Now, I know this seems convoluted. What we are doing in this moment is we are preparing a spiritual mattress, a clean, white mattress, very firm, comfortable, nothing to disturb the presence of the self as it lies there. It's a rebirthing process. So ones can feel comfortable as they transition, and by transition, I mean the heart chakra is going to open. There will be pain there. It will be like you're going to have the sense that you're dying. Well, you have already had that little piece of information. It is the opening for the healing of the, what you beings term, 144,000 selves that have been notified in your body. Everyone has them, same notification, same process, no one special in this thing. Everyone is getting it.

The knowledge that drinking the water appropriately with appropriate thought in thankfulness is, number one, immediate health to the body, because God's path is in the water. You have a lot of people messing with your water now, commercial stuff and things; the appropriateness of that is not understood yet. It is sad to say this, but eventually (well, I don't know how soon) it's going to be necessary to understand what condensation is because the disrespect for the water is pushing it away. It's an entity. It's an entity, and it has consciousness. And you're getting problems with your oceans and the pollution. The creatures are reacting, yet it is not noticed, and it's not understood.

Your planet is mostly water — saltwater, but water all over. Seventy-five percent of your planet is water. You are [about] 60 percent water. The correlation between the water in you and the water of the planet and the percentages is not truly understood. If you knew the enormity of the power you hold just within the water systems in your body, you could cure anything. You could cure anything because the path of the Creator is through there — all water. It walks there, and then you just need to learn to communicate with It and get the appropriate answers.

You do not need your preachers yelling at you. You need the ability to read, or you need the ability to hear prayers and recite them. That's what you need; that's all, nothing else. You don't need your media telling you how everybody's killing everybody; you already know that. You need to understand that space is your grace and water is your blessing.

Psalm 6 Asks for Protection Against Demonic Forces

There's going to be so much turmoil soon and pain and confusion within the body, mental disturbances, that you're going to seek more drugs, and there won't be any available. The only drug you're going to need is the knowledge of the space and the water and your proper confirmation of your foods (in other words, thankfulness for the foods that you get). Your diets are changing. Your abilities to eat like you used to eat are changing because the frequency is higher in your body now. It can't handle all that density. Your proteins, to understand what is termed the overlays and the sacredness of the animals, if you eat meat — all of these things are necessary to be considered individually of self, individually, preference, then stick to it.

This little conversation we are having now is preparatory for what we call a Pamphlet for Life. A pamphlet, a book, pamphlet. What Psalm 6 does primarily is to list your faults and ask for protection, and it primarily puts up a wall for shame to the demonic forces that are interfering with you. It asks for them to be shamed suddenly, and that's a terrifying thing out there. They are aware of it. That's the importance of that. Then you can move within a safe understanding.

Beings are being — how you say? — cursed (it's a word here, a witchcraft thing) in their dream states. In the acceptance of it or at least in the confrontation with it, you wake up and you have the confusion. So you need those prayers to prevent this. And this is occurring all over. Not many are mentioning it, but you are feeling it, and you're being introduced to it. There are demonic forces that do not like the success of the human condition. And it is success. It has come through processes, yes, but it is still the human condition, and it's the only one like it and only here. You're going to make it; we have seen. Yet it's not going to be easy.

The Purpose of This Book

When the acknowledgment of these demonic forces starts taking place and you see them and recognize them, then you're going to have a little cautionary understanding here. Someone told me, "Yes,

Psalm 6

Young's Literal Translation

6 To the Overseer with stringed instruments, on the
octave. — A Psalm of David. O Jehovah, in Thine
anger reprove me not, Nor in Thy fury chastise me.

2 Favour me, O Jehovah, for I [am] weak, Heal me, O
Jehovah, For troubled have been my bones,

3 And my soul hath been troubled greatly, And Thou, O
Jehovah, till when?

4 Turn back, O Jehovah, draw out my soul, Save me for
Thy kindness' sake.

5 For there is not in death Thy memorial, In Sheol, who
doth give thanks to Thee?

6 I have been weary with my sighing, I meditate through
all the night [on] my bed, With my tear my couch I
waste.

7 Old from provocation is mine eye, It is old because of all
mine adversaries,

8 Turn from me all ye workers of iniquity, For Jehovah
heard the voice of my weeping,

9 Jehovah hath heard my supplication, Jehovah my prayer
receiveth.

10 Ashamed and troubled greatly are all mine enemies,
They turn back — ashamed [in] a moment!

Young's Literal Translation (YLT)

I see." Then you back up, and you will hardly go back to finding another, what you call, appropriate psalm because there are others that are more significant. Psalms 148, 149, and 150 — those are the easier ones. But Psalm 6 will give you a defensive measure so that you can understand Psalms 148, 149, and 150 [see appendix].

They are basically praises to the Divine for everything. And it's the Divine that sent you, no matter where you came from or what discernment you think you are into. Just reading those provides you the ability. Those psalms — there are three particularly — are (what you say) the last sentence in the Lord's Prayer, the "For thine is the kingdom and the power and the glory forever" thing. Psalms 147, 148, and 149 relate to that thing. When you read them, you will see what that means there between the words because it's one of safety, joy, and celebration. That's what it is, because your life, the fact that you were born, number one, in your self is a cause for celebration of yourself. It always has been. And that is why beings are going through the issues that "nobody recognizes me because I'm important." But you know it's the celebration of yourself, and you are confused about why others don't have the same celebration of "you." That's what birthdays are for, to bring that memory back and to celebrate.

The celebration idea has been put off or moved by your constructs of churches to control things. But it's all going to be an individual thing now. It always has been. That's why a lot of your prophets had to go into a cave. They knew the demons were all over. They didn't want to contact or conflict. They wanted to be in a place of safety where they could have contemplation. They saw, they knew, and they felt. They just did not want to be involved. It's like you don't want to be involved with those groups because it doesn't feel good in that group. That is why Moses was sent to the desert, so he would know the difference, all of this.

You are in that now. You're going to find out that you are all prophets, pretty much, because you're picking it up. You're feeling it now. It's a mother force that introduces herself to you, that is not you, but it is you. It is like learning about a relative more. The "more" that you find out later, or now at the time, is your ancient lover's coming back. It is one where the present human condition in the body now can feel it — will feel it, will know it, will accept it, and will appreciate it in thankfulness, even though it might not be, what you call, in the physical senses as another body. But you will feel the sensation in your body as if there was another body. It's a transitional phase.

Then there's this thankfulness that occurs, and you find out it's really your higher self, or you might call it your guardian angel, but the one that has always been with you, has always loved you and will never *not* love you. And you're going through that recognition now; everyone is. The level of understanding is different. That's why there are a lot of heart attacks now going on in your young ones in their 40s, 50s, 30s, because of the misappropriation of thoughts of social consciousness. They accepted it and proved not healthy, not just the food. Thoughts kill. It is the thought that kills.

The demonstration of that is you walking your now life, watching so it is careful in this thing. Pay attention. The teachings are coming to help you heal yourself. You have to pay attention to that. Yet there are so many now who want this, what you say, group therapy, group thing there, so they can whine and whine and whine and whine. Pray. Stop. You are burying yourselves, yet that's not understood.

This is a life process book, or pamphlet. It tells you exactly what you are doing, and when you read it, you're going to realize what you did. You will see it there, and you'll know how to correct it with yourself. So it has self-judgment, self-criticism within it, and the overcoming of the doubt of the self, basically. You are going to need it after your July and later in your year. This is a tumultuous time. Basically, we and others are trying to stop World War III, really. You have the nonsense overtaking common sense. This is accepted by your leaders, and they're promoting it. They will open all the doors, and when they do, you had better know a prayer because they don't have any idea who they're calling when they do this thing.

The nuances for healing are available. The conflicts for the perpetuation of ignorance in the human condition are available. They outweigh you by probably 30 percent to 70 percent because that's what everyone is talking about. And you are not really aware of what affect your words have. You have been told and told, "In the beginning was the word." So you need to understand words manifest. You need them in the proper order for the construct of your self to be manifested through time, with time, above time — continually. So you can go in and out of time because time is a direction, and it is up. That's why you have this phrase, "Time to get up."

The Door of Total Enlightenment

The time frame's now because you have this phrase "time is collapsing." That's what you say. Space is shifting, and you're getting this collapse of consciousness. Then there will be a new one that comes up, and you are going to recognize yourself. That's what's going to happen. It'll be like … what's that tarot card with the angel blowing a trumpet and the beings coming out of their coffins, things, that one, twenty-one or something, like that, twenty-one? [See figure 1.]

You're being called, but you have to know how to answer correctly. You don't want to go into that door unprepared because it's just lightning flashing all over the place. You don't ask questions.

Your mind, you can't have a mind. You have to be in no thought. You have to be just blissing out, and you have to know how to bliss and accept, how to go up and come down. Before you go up, a robe will be placed on you for your protection. It will be placed by the Divine, the Mother, so that you don't get damaged in your own ignorance.

When you think you've learned everything and then you start having a thought, a lightning bolt will hit you because you're not supposed to think there. It's inappropriate. You were not told to talk. You have to go beyond the concept of your mind and thinking. So you go into a phase of nothingness, but you are something. You know it, because you're nothingness. That's the trick now.

Figure 1. Judgment tarot card, Rider-Waite deck

What door are we going through?

The door of total enlightenment, where you know everything and it wants all things and the satisfaction of the expression of it.

I'll take it. Is that the same as becoming a ball of light?

It is more. Basically, we are giving you spiritual survival techniques. They will be available whether you apply them or not. That is entirely up to you. But it will not be that it hasn't been said or made available.

There are very important things going on here in consciousness. Reincarnation is known. Adam became David and others in there, and Jesus is a combination of it. He gave the secrets. So we want to get that place set there and the little battles in between and all that other stuff. You're going to understand it. We are all participants in that. That's why we are recovering ourselves.

Including you?

Including me. I could tell you some stories about the angels that ... [laughs]. But we will leave that for them. There has to be interference. We tried to interfere and assist, in a manner. Some thought it was assistance, but it wasn't because the Divine knew what it was doing all the time.

Trying to help, but we didn't need ... they didn't know what to help.

We weren't assigned to help at that time, but now we're assigned to help. That's what was going on.

Okay, that's great.

You have two points in your pelvis back here, in your butt, two points. They are coming up to just behind the heart chakra. The lower back, you're getting it first. This energy is going to just come up like this. But now people are trying to bring it up out of their pelvis like this [out the front]. The pyramid goes like this [straight up].

So you have to bring it up, and what you find out is you are refining yourself. You are taking the kundalini from the left and your kundalini from your right, and you're spinning it around your spine. The third phase is like the filament that covers your bone. It's that clear-energy sheath, there, that spins the two kundalinis together. Then you have that recognition of the power, here [solar plexus], and this is where you get the acknowledgment and thankfulness of the mother force that is in the planet, the magnetic force that comes up and acknowledges you.

You're going to notice that you're going to be standing and all of a sudden your foot is going to start to stomp the ground, one of them. It doesn't matter which one. You'll feel the authority of that foot. Have you ever watched animals in nature, in your nature shows, when your antelopes, they see a lion or a tiger or something? Their foot hits the ground. [Stomps.] It's an awareness; they are stomping, warning others, and the ability to identify self [stomps]. They defend themselves. Your foot will do that, and if your foot does that, pay attention to the forces that are around you. You are calling in defensive forces when that hits because it's going to become automatic. You won't do it yourself. Someone else will do it for you and through you. That's that breath thing. You're not breathing, but you just felt that breath. [Breathes in and breathes out.] Thank you.

Is this just happening? Should we see this as a meditation, these two points coming up and down our spines? Is that interfering?

No, it's a meditation.

You can do it to assist it?

Yes. It'll spread up. It'll start here [coccyx], and once it comes up to the back of the heart chakra, you're going to feel something here [solar plexus]. It wants to open. But you need to keep it in, push it back. It wants to open. You need to come up so that it comes up here [crown chakra]. It needs to come all the way up. A lot of beings, when it starts hitting here [solar plexus], think they know everything but back up. You have more spine left, remember?

[Laughs.]

The Edge of Darkness

You said, "We have a primal power that makes us impervious to the Master of Discomfort"?

Yes. This one is the dark power. This is a black light, just at the edge of nothing, see. That's what it is.

It's still love.

Oh yes.

I mean, it's not on the dark side.

No, no. It is not what you call the dark, evil side. This is dark that knows what it's doing.

Thank you so much.

We are through.

CHAPTER

1

With Movement Comes Responsibility

July 7, 2015

The process that the human condition is going through now is, basically, the idea of names. Adam was told to name things; before that, there were no names. Gods and goddesses did not exist as names, did not exist. They were not there.

They existed, but they didn't have names? Or they didn't exist?

They did not exist. The concept of Adam being the first man needs to be understood, and the concept of creation has to be understood. The gods and goddesses evolved out of the necessities for helping humans. Part of your system of gods and goddesses were set out and manufactured, we'll say, the idea by this particular being, **Astero** the demon, was told to do this for the assistance.

Now, you may call this the original rebellion thing, the fall everyone has, that determination, you're part of it. That's the sensation you have when you fall back into your body, just a reminder, the sensation you have when you are born. It's that sort of entering into the fall; it's the fall. But you beings would term it manifesting, and the human condition is aware of its ego. It's aware of it. And it has a death-defying wish, actually, the ego does, in the permeating of all things, into the *penetration* of all things.

That condition is not conducive to the continuity of the life force that you are imbued with. The ego has a battle there with its own encapsulated light processes. It tries to dominate it. But you only can hold your breath for a few minutes, and you can only go without water for a number of days. So you are missing the conspicuousness of yourself within the breath and the water. You have completely lost it. And what you have in the human condition now are these negative forces, we will call them. I'll call them demonic, which they are because they know what they are doing, and you don't. They enter your being. They enter your being.

The Manifestation of the Cashew Tree

The first acknowledged manifestation of form from the invisible to the visible in a loving gesture for creation was a cashew, a cashew tree, the tree. The invisible force wrapped itself around the tree, squeezed the tree, created the nut, and formed the cashew, which looks like a fetus. It learned with this extreme force to form within the tree this fruit. So practice, practice, practice, practice, practice, practice, practice creation of man, the knowledge of the fruit of the nut, the fetus, to continue growth, that thing. It came from the tree. It came from the invisible force that started embracing things. That's why the force is so strong. That's why some trees are straight, and some trees are very twisted and crooked because other beings learn how to get in, and that is how the oxygen is produced for you — from the forces that want to involve themselves through.

They have to go through the tree first from the invisible to develop a consciousness of environment, number one, to develop a consciousness of the necessity. Trees have a necessity of water. There's a consciousness there that understands the need for the water from the invisible because the invisible doesn't need water. It doesn't need air. It doesn't need anything. It moves. It creates. And the blessing of the spaces that the invisible is trying to teach — what has become visible, how to do what it did from the invisible — because you all have the same capacity. You all came from the same invisible — you all have — from the same power. You all have the same knowledge if you understood who your teacher is — if you understood, as you say, the necessity of no words.

The importance of grasp, grasp, which is what the invisible did with the trees, the grasp. It understood the nature of the (how we say you?) ... we have to do it in this manner because you have the elementals. You have fire, air, earth, and water, all invisible manifested visible. The invisible-invisible, we will say, comes out of the void thing, or however you want to process that, the yin and yang. You have that knowledge of the doingness, the doing it, the doing of it. You remember that in your sleep state when you have your dream thing and you wander again. Yet the invisible light that's manifested within you in the center of your heart is visible white light; it knows. And it's, we will have to say, working backward in its memory for the appreciation that it once knew as invisible becoming visible.

At that line when the invisible becomes visible, there is a distinct acknowledgment or appreciation for the understanding of a moment different from previous moments. That is what you're working back toward. That's why we have been saying for a while to back up into your spine in your consciousness. There's all this stuff out front. You already know it is not going anywhere. You're just going to add more baggage because you just can't get rid of it fast enough. But consciously if you back up into the spinal forces, actually spinal fluid, which you can, acknowledge it, and then what happens is the bones ring. At least that is a tone there. And the tone is recognized by the invisible. The invisible being that's everywhere. It's all over on the planet. It doesn't have to go anywhere. It's like one-on-one talking to you, "Oh." When that acknowledgment starts creating the ring, you begin to develop abilities different from others.

Right now, the acceleration that is going on in consciousness is going to create a great surge in telepathy, and you're going to find out the same game is going on. It's like everyone will start throwing out their own commercials, like your TV commercials, and then you don't know what to do. You're caught up in the telepathy commercial. That's why you need to stop, back up, and listen to the invisible. You'll feel it in the bones. You'll feel it in your spine. Your meridians are being activated for the reason to hold more electrical force. You're getting (how you say?) reassembled. Part of you being taken out. We take out, and then we fix things and put back.

The taking out part creates an emotional feeling within the flesh that has been left. There seems to be an abandonment thing there. Part of you left, and confusion reigns there because the ... well, I'm going to say this: the memory packets are being readjusted. You're getting more slots, like you have your computer. You have more things here to plug things into?

Right.

Same thing what's going on now. We took things out, and we're putting in more slots. Everyone's getting in that sort of inner confirmation, physically felt, not mental confirmation. The mental will be able to understand it later. The brains are being adjusted into another frequency level so that you can understand the meaning of color and the process of color, how it relates to your interpretation of life.

You Are Feeling the Force

You're going through tonal recognition, tonal recognition. This is what's the history, but really the secret, in this phrase "the choir of angels." That's why you have choirs and churches, the singing, and the things. It changes the frequency. Your bodies are going to begin to sing. You're going to hear songs and one singing to you, what as they say, as the mother singing a lullaby. But there will not be a physical person there. There won't be anyone. There will be the natural knowledge of the truth of things, and then you begin to understand the application.

As we were singing to this one, love is forgiveness. If you really understood what that meant, you would not have an issue with what love is because, really, in the greater truth, it is none of your business what love is. You have it already. It's your misapplication, is all; you're just driving down the wrong road. And this is what is going to become acknowledged because nature now herself is stepping forth. She knows how to create. The natural force, nature on your planet, knows how to create because that's what births come from. And you have animal species now that when the nature of their environment changes, they — individually, a male and a female animal — to a certain extent, they will change sexes. A male being will become female; a female being will become male. Or they will all go female, or they'll all go male. Now, what you're seeing in actuality is that occurring on your planet in the human condition.

You have these urges in these sexual behavior things. They're feeling the force of nature. That is not a concept that you're able to understand fully in the process of your own individual unit of life.

You're given a life as an individual male entity and an individual female entity for the understanding of consciousness in form. And it was your choice in, what you call, your beginning.

But now the fear in the acceleration is coming up, and you understand these changes that are occurring within you, and you're trying to manifest them out. But you can't do that. You're going to find yourself in an inappropriate lockdown, what you say, "inappropriate place" because the communication in those circumstances becomes convoluted. You're not speaking from the tone within your bones. You've made an adjustment and accepted an adjustment from another level of consciousness that wasn't yours and had been influenced. Possession is a real thing. The knowledge of it and the dealing with it have not been taught well. There are some who understand.

You have … and it's one of the reasons you have countries with borders. Yet there shouldn't be any borders. The borders created a ball of consciousness here in "this" country, a ball of consciousness here in "this" country, a ball of consciousness here in "this" country, a ball of consciousness here in "this" country, no consciousness at all in "this" country. Over each particular country, you have a particular overlay of a particular religion or belief system. It's over each country differently, the same yet different. The process of destroying to prove that you are the one capable of being alive is a very ignorant process. That is what is occurring now because you're getting this speed up, and the radiation from the Sun is increasing. It's been, over the past year, it has increased over 200 percent.

You're not only feeling the heat of the Sun; you're feeling different rays of energy there. And what that is, is the collective group of humanity's thoughts hitting the Sun, and the Sun, in its spiritual dignity, is bringing it back to you. You're not going to like it because you can't accept that you have collectively done it. It's like the Tower of Babel thing. Humankind needs to move back through this comfort of itself, unit, skeletal structure, with appreciation. When it does, you're going to have a collapse of consciousness we're talking of. In other words, all ways are going to change almost overnight, new ideas are going to come up, and everyone is going to say, "Why didn't we think of that before?" Because you were stupid, and you didn't pay attention to anything. You're going to go through that realization, the "aha!" thing.

The barrels of thoughts and emotions that you beings ingest is amazing. You're not even aware of your ingestion process. You're just simply aware of when you eat something and drink something, you think you're ingesting. But when you're watching movies, your eyes are ingesting and interpreting and influencing and being influenced, and you've all this chemical stuff going on in you to adjust to the movies. Your space, you're ingesting everything there. You're learning to be a sponge, in a manner, and with correct petitions now, if you will, if you wish.

The human condition now is going to need to let itself be back into the mental conceptual state as if you are Adam, not Jesus. You're going to have an understanding of how to name and communicate with things, nature, in a language that is not yours. Nature is looking to communicate with you. She wants to interact through her animals, through you. The invisible comes through the animal visible form to produce your foods. Your milk and your eggs — the invisible does that for you. But you are not aware of the invisible doing it for you. It is coming to let itself know. The appreciation for the animals that produce the food should be understood as respect instead of these slaughter houses that you are doing. Human consciousness has lost it. There's no dignity there for anything, anyone — the animal nor you! This is what you're ingesting: no dignity.

As the acceleration increases — and we told you before that this July is going to be very interesting, and you're only in day seven — you're going to be thankful that you knew some prayers come August, because this month is going to cause everyone to pray something. It will. And when you get through it, you're going to acknowledge whatever prayer that was that let you get to August, or whatever being came to you, because now around your planet you have, well of course there are an exceptional number of ETs. You have a lot of disincarnate beings and ones in the higher realms here, watching this show.

The disincarnate, they are caught in a whirlpool, so to speak. They know the changes coming; they wish they had not done what they did, and they want to get back into the body to at least ride this wave because this is going to be the knowledge wave, really big one, a tsunami in your later months of this year. The tsunami is the acknowledgment of "aha!" within the self, the inspiration within the self, the confidence within the self, the safety within the self, and the idea that you are a unit for a reason. You're blessed for a reason. You just forgot it. You thought things just worked that way because your thoughts were not in the right place.

Then you're going to understand the energy of Adam, where he listened to the wind and was told even what to name the invisible and how that felt in the naming, in the process of "this" and "that" and the "other." Then you're going to find those beings who are here yet not here, that are not a part of the human condition but that are interacting with you in a way that is not appropriate, as you would term it. Yet in the appropriateness of it, they're getting you back on track. You're eventually learning, or will learn, what evil is. The first step you could at least inculcate or contemplate is that murder is illegal, illegal. It's beyond illegal. It's evil. When you understand that, then you will understand the consciousness that develops that capacity to do that, and the healing process will begin. The new cashews begin to be formed.

Recognize the Nature of Your Inappropriateness

You are in an experimental stage of creatorship. You are. The first step of that is shaman school. You've heard the word "shamans" and what they are supposed to be able to do, and "this-that," communicating with nature and enlightening and calming space and walking differently. The metaphysical community now is being interviewed, and those being interviewed are being interviewed for a particular schooling. That schooling is the school of a shaman, the mental capacity of the true understanding of the self with air and water. That is what it is. And it is the acknowledgment of your own, we are going to use this word, which is a word beings don't like, the acknowledgment of your own "sinful" behaviors — sinful behavior, sinful behavior. Once you understand that, you can correct yourself. You don't need anyone to tell you. You already know it. You knew the laws; you disobeyed them. All humans have, and you know it. You knew it as a little one.

Now is the process to get back and forgive, and love is the forgiveness. So you love yourself for that moment, even if they knew you were sinful, you love yourself to forgiveness and go forth. And it is an emerald-green energy, this love. Emerald green is the energy of St. Michael. He cried emeralds when this thing fell apart, and that is why he is a protector. You are going to understand that frequency and the importance of it within the self for healing.

The reason beings don't want to be healed is they think they're doing penance, and they are enjoying that suffering, on a level. They can grab other people around them to suffer with them and pray for them because they don't want to pray. It's going to come to a point where there won't be ones to pray for you. They are going to be too busy praying for themselves, and the prayer is you just have to acknowledge God, whatever that word means to you. Whatever name it brings — whatever, ever, because that is your rescuer. You have no one else, none, because you've never communicated with them. You didn't want to, so they don't want to pay attention.

You come from a spiritual line now, and that calling back to the perfection of that line is what is occurring. You've heard of the being called Thoth, eh? That being is, what you would term, the Archangel Gabriel, and he's aware of Osiris, Isis, Anubis, and the others and understands the idol built to incorporate that image, that energy. It was told to do it for a reason. They were termed the false gods, yet in the understanding of lordship, you have to tend to the flock a little bit to learn about the flock, and that's what they were doing, all right.

There is a reclamation process going on with that too right now, and that's why some beings can say some things and some beings can say nothing. They are coming under a jurisdictional influence. You must understand that the words that you have in your ancient books, your Bible, your Torah, and these things, were written by beings who would interpret a word and can put together the letters of the words. Yet in the moment of things — the receiving of the information through ones and transmitting it to ones who could write — it was a long process and a confusing process, and the one who wrote along the way made interpretation, which shouldn't have been done. It should have been left the way it was said because of the importance of the space between the words. That never happened, and that's why you have all of this now.

Well, it's all going to be (how you say?) ashes, we'll say, in a concept. Your books are going to sort of go away, burn up, and soon you'll be left with nothing, in an allegorical sense, because your ability to know this new language that is coming is going to be different. You're going to feel a different language. You are going to speak differently. You're even going to feel beings coming in and saying something through you, and you didn't say it. So you have to know the line of your thought and continuity, where you're going. Well actually, you're not going anywhere.

You're descending in this ascension process if you want to stay alive. You can ascend, which is die the body, one way, or you can take the body into light. But that hasn't been done often here. Or you can descend with it and be corrected because you will — because your posture and your process and your thoughts aren't correct — have to excuse yourself at times for being inappropriate. We like that word "inappropriate" instead of "ignorant." You're just inappropriate; you just don't understand yet. So you did something inappropriate for the space and time.

That nature of inappropriateness is not understood. It's not understood. This is what's causing the great requirement from the spiritual realm to loved ones down here. It's causing them agony to love down here because you're doing everything inappropriately. And pretty soon there's going to be a big broom that is going to clean up the store because you're seeing it all in your news, and you're seeing it everywhere. The dysfunction of this condition is going to become more apparent, and that is when everyone starts screaming for life. They'll beg for the sorry from within themselves and for mercy, and they'll change. The opportunity to change now is magnificent. You have great portals opening; many things are in your consciousness. Many things have been presented in your movies and, what you would say, the abilities of certain functions were given to beings. They've displayed it in your cinemas, so at least when it really begins to happen, you have some idea, not really a great one, but some.

Control through Remote Viewing

You have, what your word is, governments manipulating your consciousness now with the thought streams. They're very … these … how you call these beings?

Sinister Secret Government?

Well, your government, particularly. You have beings (what you say?) that look into the future.

Oh, pre-cogs, prophets ... um ... ?

No, not the ...

Psychics?

It's a military thing.

Oh! Remote viewing.

Yes. They've been stopped there. They're going to a certain place where they can influence arenas from the remote-viewing aspect, and right now, you are being influenced by remote viewers. It wasn't all, as you say, to gather information. It's more than that. It was to control and manipulate and influence consciousness and great units — areas — of consciousness. That's why there was prevention, and they couldn't see further.

Oh, they were prevented by the spiritual forces, now you're saying?

Yes.

Ah, I didn't get that.

Now they are living in their mess, and they are trying to clean it up, but they can't. There's an attempt to start a race war here. This is not even intelligent. So you're getting old, very old, energies coming up in a chance to say (how you say?) these are ...

Yes, we did that fifty years ago! What's going on? Yeah.

You have these beings who are spiritual entities who die in a war, say, or die, and they're still floating around the planet, but they're still in the warlike-energy thing. As your planet evolves, so too do the spiritual forces within that planet, but they still have these desires and wants for justice, sort of thing, and there's possession going on here. The more you can get people confused and angry over "this" thing and "that" thing, you're going to create this antagonism instead of building together to understand things. But this ...

That's what they're doing?

That's what they're doing. That's what they're doing, and they're using the spiritual forces of the planetary alignments as they come in now because they know how to manipulate them. You're all influenced by it. You look at it, "That's pretty." But what does it do? How is it affecting you? What's the message there?

How do we protect ourselves?

Pray. You have (again a couple of nights ago) what you would term the Star of Bethlehem showing up in the sky, in the sky.

A couple of nights ago? So about the Fourth of July?

Yeah.

What is the Star of Bethlehem? What do we call it?

Well, you call it the Star of Bethlehem that signals the birth of Jesus, basically.

I know, but what star are we looking at?

It's not really a star.

What is it?

It's a being.

Oh, a being ... ?

Metatron. Well, let me put it this way. It's the being behind Metatron.

Who is that?

El Shaddi, the being with two horns on its head that all creatures bow before when he shows up. Part of the difficulty here is warning the human condition about what's about to occur.

Without scaring them.

Also, allowing the consciousness within the system of the individual unit to prepare itself as best it can without fear. The consciousness that is showing up is the one that activated your bones, the one that activates your bones from the beginning, before you had bones, that gave you bones and gave you the need for the bones as a walking human. With movement — and this hasn't been truly understood in the human condition — (the ability to move) comes responsibility because you affect things. Even kicking a rock creates a change somewhere down the line, actually all over the planet. So when you understand movement and thought, you become a little more pristine, more aware of the effect of your movement on others, and you're cautious, not trying to affect others in a negative way. You're not clumsy.

You're not going in like a bull into the china shop. But you're all acting like that, walking bulls, walking around not caring because you're you, and you can do what you want. That's the idea that has caught the human condition in a situation now. That's why this energy of fear is around. That's why everyone's feeling it. They don't know where to go for comfort yet. They don't. As your abilities to meditate change, some are going to find out they've been meditating on the wrong thing because it's going to have an effect on the physical body, literally.

You Cannot Advance until You Understand Why You Are Here

You are in a stage now where you are becoming, from a cashew in a fetus, another form of living being with a more purposeful intent and not a fearful mentality about it. You're going to start listening to the back of your skull, back of your head. Within the inside of your skull, you are going to allow the eyes of you to see, from inside you, the heavens, the stars that are there, and that's why you recognize the stars out there because you have them in the back of your head. When the connections between the spinal column and the stars in your head align — and you understand where you came from and what you are doing here, why you are here — you will understand that you have taken another step, not only here but out there from where you came from. You can't advance out there until you understand what you are doing here.

Wow!

Did you get that one?

Yeah [laughs].

That's the stage you are in now. The part of you that is out there is waiting for you to complete here, in a manner, where you're still conscious, so all of you can advance out there with the acknowledgment of that advancement. Along with that comes responsibility and power. Power comes first, then the responsibility. That's what you're in now because those beings who know things are supposed to do things with what they know, not just simply manipulate. You're here to heal. You are on this planet to heal.

Things done in the past and things being done in the present and things that might be done in the future, you're to create a healing space. There are always hospitals in war zones somewhere. You're in a war zone now, and your hospital is in your spiritual realm. That's where you can seek your comfort because the human condition doesn't know anything right now. You are repeating the same stuff. It's a repeat, a repeat, a repeat.

But deliberately influenced to be a repeat?

Until you get it, yes. You keep falling down until you get up and walk.

So there is a purpose behind it? These beings who are manipulating it: In the long run, they're trying to teach us?

Yeah, there it is, because the only ones who are really qualified will make it through here. It's like a spiritual boot camp. You're going through it, and everyone's getting weeded out. The first weeding is the shamans' school. Everyone's being trained in some level of shamanship. You're going to know it because you are going to start appreciating nature more now and communicating more with nature and trusting what she says, the animals and how they behave, and other things. Then the shaman energy starts coming together, and the shamans start working together in a different way that you haven't understood yet. It's a way in the ethers, three levels and things, colors. Just by thinking of colors, you could connect to another shaman who works with the same colors. You're in the same frequency.

You have a lot of beings now who are enjoying the dark forces because they can see and feel the sense of power there. But the body consciousness has a (how you say?) feeling it likes, the power there, but it doesn't understand it's losing its innocence or it's a perception of what is pure; we'll put it that way.

One of the sad things to say is when things start falling out of the sky on you that you haven't seen before and they look, in a manner, like metallic … metal, that means that this energy has lowered its frequency to manifest in a density that is recognizable by you; that's all. They don't need these forces around them for them to exist. Yet in your world, they need them because of the violence that is down here on your planet and the reaction of your forces and things.

By "they," you mean extraterrestrials?

Yeah. They are delicate. You can't hug an extraterrestrial like you can hug a human. You could kill it, and the aggressiveness of the human nature and its things are why they have this demonstration of their ability to project force — its ability to do. They can do it. But they are under jurisdictional laws also. You have some really evil groups of consciousness located in countries on your planet. It is simply evil because it will not allow anyone any free thought of any movement or anything. It's a totally controlling force, and that force seeks domination here, so you have a controlling force here, and you have other countries here but not so controlling. They are going to need to be controlling to get a hold of this one, to settle it down; otherwise you're going to have problems you don't even want to consider.

I will say this, and no one's said it. We ask that it doesn't happen, but there is a place on your world today that, literally, is a black hole, and if it's not adjusted, everything is going to collapse within it. You have heard of the power of black holes. Well, you have one developing on your planet Earth right now. That's why you are having an exceptional amount of extraterrestrial activity coming, because if this planet goes into a black hole, it's going to suck everything, including your Sun and all the other planets around it, in it. That's what's happening here in consciousness on your Earth today — now! But you don't recognize it.

The evil consciousness is creating this black hole?

Yeah, it is; it's coming up from the center of Earth.

Deliberately?

Deliberately! It is raising others in power so that they can perpetuate the negativity. You call it negativity, but it's evil.

But they don't understand the danger?

No, they don't care. It's like the feeling of power for humans.

But it would suck them in just like us.

Oh yes, but they think they're going to be allowed not to.

I see.

They are not very bright. But it's worse than a sickness. It's worse than a sickness, and what it is you are going through now, I might as well say it, is the extinction of you. Hmm. It won't be pleasant. That's the battle going on now, literally. It's not a figment of your imagination. It's not. So you need to prepare yourselves in your consciousness of your spinal column of who you truly are.

You're like a tree, and that is the symbol of the Anunnaki as they are coming. They show you; from a basket, they are feeding you fruit, for you're part of them, part of their line, children will say. They're not here to do damage. They're here to help. But no one wants it because you have your own belief systems, and when your own belief system is shattered, you have no idea what to do. This is what the human condition is going through. They have no one to look for, to look up to. They are entertaining themselves with their television because they need to see something and know something, but that something out there is not what you really need to know.

You should establish a communication, and the best way to do that is you have a bowl of water that you use at night with the Moon, and you communicate with the Moon. You talk to the water. The Moon will talk to the water, and you refresh yourself. At least then you are getting some information. You don't have to confirm it. You can confirm it with the Sun in the morning. The Moon is a reflection of the Sun's energy; you know that. The Sun reflects your thoughts, so if the messages coming back are kind of convoluted, check your thoughts in the morning as you go to the Sun because your answers come back in the Moon. Hmm?

Now, you have another frequency that you're not aware of yet, and I know this is kind of long, we have been talking. You have this frequency of the Moon and the water, the Moon and the water. The Moon comes closer. The water moves, so you say. Yet as the Moon comes closer, the water moves it. It comes in to push the Moon away with its force. As it does, the Moon goes away — high tide, low tide. It goes to the other side, and the Moon comes back. So the water and your Moon are significant communicators, really. And you can use it; you can use it. You can understand it.

There is an electrical force that flows through the water continuously. It doesn't stop. If you could just barely touch your finger on the surface of the water, you could feel it singing. Communicate. You could set up your own communication at the Moon. You can have two bowls of water — one for the right hand, because of the level of consciousness in your right hand, and then the one for the left hand. There's a level of consciousness in the left side of your body. Then you have a third bowl that you put both hands in. So you can understand your left self, your right self, and your middle self. The middle self is the one that is trying to hold you all together. Then you will understand your spiritual self. Then you'll understand why Shiva had a little bowl of water there in front of him with the Moon above his head. You will understand what that means. So you're in this process now.

Connect to the Stars for Assistance

As far as all of this information we have given today … usefulness. How do we work with the usefulness of this? How do we get it so that beings don't become fearful in understanding this yet acknowledge your own presence as you are going through it? How do we do that?

You all know, heard, of the Tree of Life. You all heard of prayers. You all heard of color and sound. You all heard of notes and the tones in your bones. So you need to get a little register [metronome] and go through the notes, A, B, C, D, E. Find one that is yours that resonates from the top of your head to the bottom of your feet all at the same time, just one note. Focus on that. That's part of your life stream, part of your initial vibration of self, and you need to do it in a quiet manner without influence from other beings.

Okay, now are there any questions?

How do we connect from the spinal fluid in the brain to the eyes in the back of the head?

When that fluid moves up, you will get an acknowledgment right here in the jawbone. There will be a tendency to open the jaw and the feeling to speak, and you don't speak.

That's that atmospheric pressure?

Yeah, well, everyone's going through it, eventually. But as it comes up, what will happen is you will find yourself in …

Like in an airplane?

Yeah, but in an auditorium [planetarium], so to speak, with stars in the roof [ceiling], and you'll feel it. And a particular star will light up in the back of your head, and it will be in conjunction with the star that you will see out there because these are where they really are. They're not out there; humanity is projecting them out there, all right. It is a hologram for the human condition. You understand the terms "galaxies" and "supernovas" and all those things that are way out beyond, beyond, but the human condition has been gifted in the creator status that it creates. That's what you're doing. You're still doing it.

When the stars light up in your head, in the back, here, you're going to align with a particular star, and a particular star has a jurisdiction. Sirius, you're aware of those, Orion and the stars in Orion, and you're aware of the Pleiades. You've seen the beings from the Pleiades, that star system. These are graduating placements. You have heard the story of how the Pleiades were placed in the sky, okay, those kinds of things, and you're going to understand your connection. The love that these stars have for you is incredible; you just don't understand it. It's there, all forever, and they're very concerned, the energy there, particularly the Seven Sisters, the Pleiades. They are here to assist. Yet no one is really listening. Or they'll listen and say and do a little bit but not much. Don't get the idea that there is not an argument among the stars; there is. There is confusion and conversation, we'll say.

About humanity?

About a lot of things, about a lot of things, just about everything — that's what keeps things going, basically. So your conditions now, here, are going through here. You are going to go through pretty outrageous changes, as when these beings begin to manifest — I am talking about the spiritual beings now that are coming — they step on the sky, and they create a sound. Usually before they come, you will hear a sound, like trumpets or those sorts of things, and that's a prelude to their coming. That's not them; they're not there yet. Then you'll hear or feel the space shake and the earth move. It won't be an earthquake; the space will shake above the earth. Then the earth will shake; you will feel that. That will be the acknowledgment that there is a difference working here. That's what's about to occur in your September-October area.

You're going through it now; emotionally you are already feeling it. That's why everybody's spooky [spooked]; you don't know what you're doing. You're forgetting one moment to the next — what you did, what you're going to do. What day is it? We have told you that time is a direction, and it's up. You are going to understand what that means as you ascend into the pyramid of your soul, which is in the body. It's not about you yet. The base of that soul is going to drop below your feet, and the apex is going to go above your head. You will be a three-sided pyramid, and then you will be joined by other forces, which give you the icosahedron, or whatever you call it. The Sri Yantra form is what you call it. You're moving into a … ability …

Oh, the pyramid becomes a Sri Yantra?

Yeah. Yeah, you have ones going up and others coming down. It's a wedding.

Like a Star of David?

Well, there are seven of them. There is one more, three up and three down, and then you become the merkabah, actually, the Sri Yantra. You work it.

You said what will happen when the fluid moves up to join the eyes in the back of the head and how we would feel the pressure in our ears, but is there anything we can do? That just happens? We don't try to force it or accelerate it?

No, you couldn't force it. It is a permission-given thing.

We can't. Okay, we just acknowledge that it happens?

Yeah. The solar plexus is what will be the activator there. The solar plexus and then your sternum get it because the sternum has to take most of the energy and the ribs.

CHAPTER

2

When You Understand Descension, You Don't Have to Climb the Mountain; the Mountain Comes Down to You

July 14, 2015

As you begin the process of knowing yourself, it occurred with the first breath out of the womb, and because the brain — the physical brain in the newborn baby — is so clear and clean, unfettered by social consciousness input, it is excitedly the brain itself. It excitedly receives input and distributes it through the system, and it realizes the reaction from that input in the action of the body and reflexes.

So the brain itself is practiced as you first come out of the womb. It is not aware of the influence in the mental processes of those adults around. It's not aware of that. It is aware of the intent of its birth as it bore itself — was born, pushed out as the God force pushes — and it became aware of its unique position in the cosmos. This is just as you come out of the womb into a new expression. While you're in the womb, you're under the influence of tone and sound — tone and sound being both the same category, but tone has an influence where it is pleasant. Sound can be discordant. But tone and music and the bones understand that your manifested physical portion allows you to be vertical. The clues for that — information about the bones — are in your holy books.

How You Manifest on Earth

In this time and age, 2015, the beings are learning the process (very basically) of direct manifestation. Right now you breathe and eat and drink water to stay alive. Those are the concepts of your idea of direct manifestation in the physical world. In the other world, you descend self and are manifested, and the physical portion that requires air, water, and food learns to breathe appropriately, drink the appropriate water, eat correctly — little bit here, little bit there. You don't need your big fat meals every three hours. You need to understand that light descends, and you're ascending as light. So that incorporation helps align the system, the seven chakras. That is your system; the seven chakras are your system.

The heart and the lymphatic system and your liver and your organs are all manufactured out of the same seed, different direction. The idea of concepts of manifestation and how they work — the semen in the egg is all you have, and everything else comes out of that.

Tone is in the bones, the tone of yourself, or we could say it this way: The tones of you are in the bones. Each chakra has a different tone, so of course we are including them all. You're going through that process of learning, number one. The grace and dignity you have been given as life, it stands now, as you don't know how you did it. You understand the concept of coming in from reincarnation, but you don't understand the body formation. You were given one. And the idea of being given a body, receiving a body, and being blessed with the body is not solidified in the human condition, because the ones in the body think they're the body. And you have (we'll say) invited visitors into your flesh system by thinking inappropriate thoughts when you are eating, thinking inappropriate thoughts when you are breathing, and thinking inappropriate thoughts when you are drinking water. All those influences are inappropriate. You know what they are because you want to experience it, but you are not aware of where that influence is coming from. The human condition thinks it's so brilliant that it knows everything and just continues walking in the mud.

You have beings from the other realms influencing you continuously for their motivation and gratification and benefit, not yours. So as you align the self and you consider the tone in your bones, you will get another reaction to yourself because your particums and particles collectively gathered, magnetically and electrically functioning as a unit called the self. That is what you are doing literally, going on and off. You're like the zeros and ones in the computer language. Zero is off and one is on, and you go off and on. You blink so fast that you can't perceive it, and that's why you beings get so caught up in your words and conversations. Everyone's looking for someone to explain what forgiveness of the self is.

The tone is in your bones. You are your tone; you need to connect. The purpose of meditation initially was to get you into a subtle state in which you are not influenced by (what you term) negative entities and you are in protected space and set your itinerary. By "setting your itinerary," I mean collecting space, and I will call it that for this demonstration. You collect space from the time you wake up into your noon; there's a space. What you do in that space ... and then you have another space, noon to your three, and you collect; you do something there. Now you're noticing in your three to four there's an energy. There's a tiredness, and there's a rest frequency. There's a slow down, and this is where you should participate in the understanding that there's something different going on here.

In your time frame, regardless of what time zone you're in, between three and four, you can feel it. You need to acknowledge it. You need to ask what it is. It's not being influenced by HAARP; it's not being influenced by the government. It is not being influenced by anything like that. It's being influenced by the nature of the Moon and you. I don't mean by the phase of the Moon. I mean, the nature of the Moon.

The Moon has a very strong emotional attachment with the human condition. The Moon was a witness to what we understand in your world and the interpretation of the crucifixion, and you're feeling that energy there of the force that tried to overturn the teachings of the masters. That's what you're feeling. But it didn't succeed, because the teachings of the masters are still here.

Everyone knows that name; everyone knows other names. And now you're going through the process where (you call the entity) Jesus talked about Mohammed coming, and you have the influence of the Mohammed coming through in your culture now. In this tradition in the East, the entity Jesus was establishing what you call a place of peace, for he knew the coming of what you are going through now. The Archangel Gabriel is the one who gave the Koran and communicated with Mohammed. He's the (we'll call it) guardian of space, as you term it.

Health to the body, mind, and spirit. Health to the Buddhas, health to the bodhisattvas. The force that's moving across your planet does not want to start another religion — you have a religion here, religion there — it wants to unify the whole thing. You find out that Earth itself is your religion. You're going to have to learn to communicate with her. And that force comes up from the back through the pelvis and up the skeletal structure.

Where? Any specific place in the pelvis?

Initially it triggers up through the bottom of the chakras on the feet, but the real hit will come into the buttocks. It will come in and try to go up.

Get Back to the Beginning

There is a spirit within the space that moves the consciousness rivers for those willing to swim in a clean stream. There are those who don't know what a clean stream is because they are accepting the wordings of others without understanding their own words, or wordings, because in the beginning of you, there was the word. What you really need to get into in meditation is the moment of your conception — where your father and your mother met. You need to meditate into that point regardless of what violent or loving or nurturing action, whatever. You need to get to that point because that's where you came through.

Even through the mental process of your descent, you thought you were going to get away with all these things. You thought because "this" happens, and you anticipated and you planned, but it doesn't work out that way, because your manifestors in this reality were your physical parents. They were your creators in the understanding of bones and flesh — not the capacity of the ego and (what you call) the reincarnational aspects that come in, but they're your manifestors. That's where you learn that your parents, as you grow up, are not God because your understanding of God is much greater than those two. It's the arguments and things with the generations and all that — all that confusion and things. Everyone growing up as a child has gone through things, emotional impacts and things, with your creators on this planet, who are your mother and your father. Simple, that is what happened.

The realization is that you get put through this process of more divinity. You find out you have another mother and a father because you came from somewhere by another creator force or creatrix force, but you don't know which one. You come in as rainbows. You come in on rays of light. They could be dark or bright; they could be white, green, yellow, orange, or blue light beams. The tone is in your bones.

When you figure and contemplate the self of the tone in your bones behind the heart chakra and without judgments on your parents at all — any judgments — you find that moment of action when the seed left your father and entered the womb of your mother, the egg. You're there! You will either perceive yourself as semen swimming to the egg in the male constructs or an egg receiving the semen. Either one, it is what has determined your sexuality — your male or female presence. That's what determined it, that moment you are witnessing and experiencing.

Now, the semen, as it comes, there are many seeds there, all swimming and becoming competitive in racing to the egg. The egg is sitting receptively, waiting and anticipating. That's the creative consciousness; the seed has no idea. It doesn't know; it's just swimming to get somewhere. Basically, it knows it needs to get to the egg as a cave to be safe. Out there in the swimming seas, it's (what you say) dangerous, and the cave, safe.

So when you get to that point in your meditation, you will know, number one, a great idea of who you are, and number two, you will understand your purpose in accepting and entering a unified consciousness, which is the egg and the sperm. That's a unified consciousness, that right there — unified not only with the desire of the mother, for intrinsically it's the mother who sends up prayers (we'll say), or thoughts, you call them thoughts (whatever it is), but it's prayers. They end up being prayers — or they will be — because it is a manifestation involved in the thoughts of the father uniting. It's the mother's prayer that is held within the egg that you answered in your courageous form in what you call the nonexistence of self, but it exists in a dark void (you term it the void) that attracted you for the expression for assistance. It also would benefit you because you would get another physical body, and you would understand the nature of your perpetuosity, we'll call it, your perpetual nature, your foreverness. You live forever somewhere, somewhen.

This is the time on your planet — 2015. You're figuring this out. That's why there's so much turmoil, because no one really has an idea. You want to change the thought, and the tone through your bone changes because you can get back to that point, the union of the egg and the sperm; you've grown up through it — body grows up, parents, all that stuff. But you get back there, and you forgive yourself — and your parents — for being overaggressive at times. You thank your parents because you have a self now.

As you study more the doctrine of Spirit (and that really hasn't been given, but it is talked about all over the place) and you begin to understand it, then you know what a precious and sacred being you are. But you are not more holy than anyone else, just a little bit more cautious in who you're going to follow and what thought streams you're going to heal your body with. The tone is in the bones, and the healing occurs through the bones due to the correct resonance.

The Reflection of Consciousness in the Human Condition

All humans have their own songs that they answer to. It's a calling. And what you're experiencing now in your world, nature is starting to pay more attention to you in your communication abilities. You're not recognizing it yet because the human condition is too violent. But as you slow it down — and I don't mean violent like animals, you would say, get violent when they attack another animal for food, yet that is another avenue, another condition (humans are supposed to understand that) — there is a shift going on in nature, and its recognizing the spirit of things and the requirement for things and the obligation of things.

Everyone on your planet here has a firm foothold, but you also have obligations. Those things kind of frighten people: the obligation or the ability to create peace. That's one of the hardest things to do on your planet because when there's a peaceful state, there is usually a sense of bliss that you don't have to do anything right now. You can slow down and calm things down, and space adjusts itself, and then the creatures within it adjust. But there's this need. A fear comes because you have recognized things you haven't done not only a couple days ago or weeks ago but *years* ago. And that's what's coming up now in the reflection of your consciousness in the human condition.

Beings are thinking back through their lives now and trying to stabilize a natural presence. The health of the organism requires delicate care, and by that [organism], I mean Earth. It's an organism just as much as you are an organism. It has a consciousness, it has feelings, and it reflects and projects. Yet at the present time, it does not speak to everyone.

There is an occurrence beginning to manifest itself. People are interested in becoming very enamored with crystals in the crystal skulls and all these stones. Before planet Earth can communicate to you, because its voice is very loud and resolving, it vibrates all space. You can imagine. You learn to communicate with crystals and stones, yet now you think they have more wisdom than you, been around longer, but they don't move. You have to carry them from place to place. You are the one who is supposed to be moving and balancing the planet. You're the one who is supposed to be talking to the stones and telling *them* what to do, not listening to the stones telling *you* what to do. You're supposed to be calming the space, yet that is not occurring.

Everyone is running around trying to excite the space just so that they can pretend to be doing something. The doing of something is understanding: eat correctly, drink correctly, and drink your water with the blessings, and then you are protecting the space. Space then shifts, literally, like a Rubik's cube when you twist those things. Yes, like that, and they are cubic. They just know the agreement within the cubes to be within a particular portion of space, and the entity will shift it. When it shifts it, it doesn't take hands. It doesn't take hands; it takes an electrical current.

All you need is a good shot of lightning on your head, and then you'll have a good idea of difference. But I don't recommend it. You're a composite entity: You are an electrical being, and you are a magnetic being at the same time. The tone of those two frequencies is in the center of your spine, the tone of you. The first hint of the tone is in your name, particularly the first letter of your name. That's your start of your beat and the tone in your bones, not the beat of your heart. The significance of that first letter, just pronouncing it, humming it, saying it inside yourself, creates a new idea of you. If your name were Beth, you would contemplate the *B* and understand the *B* before the "eth." That is your beginning, and then you would find yourself going back to how it was selected and given as an input for force for memory of self, because if you didn't have your name, you wouldn't have an idea.

You might have, how you say, the expression of it, but the name gives you a melody for the bones to understand and for your original tone to be recognized as you. You're a tone, a tone in the celestial scheme of things. You're a song. You don't sing verbally. You are sung and are doing the singing, yet you're not verbalizing it. You are literally a tone, and before that tone, there's an intent. That is where the human condition is looking backward: its original intent — intent for manifestation, intent for physical incarnation. Why the intent? What was the intent before the intent? And then the sounds and the colors come, and you are here.

You are going into that process, and part of that process is learning to live in forgiveness because you're going through — everyone knows, you each know what you've done; you know what you've hidden — a time (pretty soon) when everyone is going to know what everyone else has done. That's the danger because they are going to get caught up in the judgment of it. Don't. Believe me, they're having enough problems with their own judgment on these things because it's going to be an open mirror for everyone then. I said "open mirror." There's no reflection. Between the mirror there is an open space, and then in that grouping, everyone will be, number one, forgiving themselves and forgiving everyone else.

There won't be an idea. Everyone will be sitting in what is termed a circle of angels, I would say, and then you will find out that you were told to go here and told to go there and told to do that. You do it because you have an expertise that's needed there. That's why you were sent. That's why you were sent. You were sent! In the answering of the prayer of your mother, you were sent.

You don't remember who sent you, but you remember being sent because you fell and you came to be born. Everyone had all these ideas, those who remember something — "It was supposed to be this way. It's supposed to be that way. It didn't ..." — because you were sent to that time and space for a function because that time and space was not working appropriately in the new idea of things to come, as all time and space is not appropriate. It's not working appropriately because you have a phrase here called humankind. But you are not kind. Humankind is not kind. It's not.

You Are Being Prepared for a Dignified Force

There's a fear running rampant now. It's being promulgated by all your politicians, rumors of all countries that don't know what to do because the populace is in trouble. There's not enough money, so you say. You were caught. The human condition has been caught, and now you're waiting for someone with all the money to come and just give it away so that everyone will be happy. That's not going to happen.

You're in this. You're literally in a struggle for the definition of the continuity of the human condition. There are those who want to take the human condition off the planet completely and just allow this to be a nature kingdom — no human condition interfering with the natural flow of nature, no dams stopping the water, no borders, animals can roam freely wherever they know how to go to be. But the human condition has messed it up. There are those who want to completely remove the human condition from this sphere. But that's not going to happen, because there are some in the human condition who understand the sacredness of nature. That is what is to occur here, and that's the struggle you're going through now, literally.

The feelings in your news media and everything — the

promulgation of it, the realization — will hit. You will all back up through the tone in your bones and understand why you are really here, why you were sent. You were sent because you had an expertise in some manner, or at least the capacity to learn about that expertise, because you've been around for a very long time in many realms. You have taken experiences from many realms, all of you have, and brought them here for what? We know that you thought you might get away with something here (little bit "there," little bit "here") and perhaps do something. But now the "do something" is what's important. The doing of it — something. Even if you're sitting in your chair meditating, you're doing something.

Yet it should be for the space around you first so that you can understand the great dignity that's coming. This is a dignified force. It knows it. The forces that are preceding it, before it arrives, know it. And the human condition is being prepared for it, and those who are (how you say) perceptually aware can feel it. They are willing and wish to participate. This is a decsension — a descension — of the Holy Spirit upon humankind in conjunction with the Spirit of Space, two different forces unified within the human condition. Once that's understood, your sickness goes away. Why? Because you realize you are dying yourself, and you know what you're doing.

It's a manner of self-inflicted suicide, negative thinking. You think you're better off somewhere else, and you don't appreciate even where you're at. Yet the movement of somewhere else will, what you say, come about in the manner when you recognize the true movement of yourself, the need to be a place more for others than for self, because that's the nature of things and a safe way.

The human condition has been so trained in fear-oriented consciousness that the gentleness is having difficulty coming out.

Gentleness is trained (how you say?) in the manner of social behavior: criticism, control, manipulation. All that's going to change. It will be like floating on the water. You are going to learn that you are the director of the current within that water because it's been said before that God walks through the water.

There is a force beyond this phrase called God. Those are words for you. There's a dignity that is beyond dignity, and it acknowledges itself within that dignity everywhere and everywhen. It knows who it's willing to teach, a more dignified presence. It does. They do. And those willing to learn are being sought out and gently being guided.

Your Bones Sing

Your tone of self, the true self, is in the vertebrae right behind the heart chakra. That's the tone there when it's realized, and as music, certain notes go together and are very pleasant. Certain tones go together very harmoniously; that is what is going to occur in the unification of the human condition. Tones are going to associate with tones harmoniously. You're going to really understand that you are musical beings, yet the voice is not your only form of music. Your bones sing. And when they sing, they vibrate. When they vibrate, light permeates and goes through them. Then it starts shining through you. So you have found the secret of yourself. It's manufactured in your marrow where blood is manufactured, and the tone in the bone creates that continual manufacturing of blood. That's what the Holy Spirit rides upon and blesses you with continually, yet the human condition does not appreciate that understanding.

Just clapping your hands [claps hands] puts a tone in your bones of appreciation for yourself. You clap your hands for everybody else. Clap your hands for yourself because you're privileged to be here. Everyone physical on this planet, even those who are suffering in the most undignified places, understand it is a privilege here. They got here to experience something at least, even for a moment. Even newborns who die — who come through, have that expression breath, and within a couple of days, they decide not to be here and leave — there's another process going on here. If the prayers were correct, those little ones would not have left. Pretty soon humans are going to understand what dignity is. You haven't defined it, yet you have it in your dictionary. But you're not living it. You have no idea. It doesn't mean a table with knives and forks set out pretty with little flowers and you can just sit there so precisely. That's not it.

Actually, we're moving. You have noticed the energies this month. We talked about this, yet your August is going to be a little gentler, and during your September, you'll be breathing, wondering, "How did I make it through that? That was crazy." That'll be the thing. Then you're going to really understand. Those vertebrae *behind* the solar plexus — in back of the solar plexus — are probably one of your most powerful signatures of presence that you have in the body, not counting the cervical and the crown when it starts opening, but interiorly here as you're going up.

At the solar plexus in those vertebrae back there is the knowledge of how to push force, how to bring it back and send it back up. When the solar plexus opens like a big cannon, you can really push force through that thing and physically affect someone. You want to bring it back in, put it back in there, and that helps open the chakras behind the shoulder blades. That's where you're angelic force comes through and displays that way. It's for you to understand the safety of yourself now. The cadre units of consciousness in spiritual warriors, we will say, those conditioned for this manner, are being set here, here, here, being set. Why? For protection of those who wished to continue in the understanding of the dignity of humankind. That's what's going on. That is what is going on.

You're feeling the energy of it this month, July, before it hits consciousness. So now that you're feeling it, you need to back this up and calm it down, because you know it's not calm. Everyone knows it isn't. It is up to everyone individually. Slow this down — slow this down — because you're running hell-bent over the cliff like a bunch of lemmings. You're really going for that cliff. And we'll see what happens toward the end of your month of July here, how far you go and whether you go over the cliff. Well, you went over the cliff. Then you're going to need to find someone to pray again for conception, and you'll be sent to it. Otherwise, you'll be floating around in the astral with all the other beings who think they can influence you but can't now.

Everybody's been put in their place for peace whether they like it or not. And there's a lot of complaining going on. Now, the healing formation of yourself — well, I won't go there. We'll let it stand as it is. The motion of emotion can be modified within the concept within the tone of the bone of you, your self. And you're going to find out it's your dark self that knows this. The black self (what you call your self) comes out of the void wrapped in a black cloak. It's to cover the light so that you don't destroy everything that is what it is. If you pull that off, you're knocking people down. So you're covered in a cloak for that reason, because you have no idea yet what you are doing — because if you did, in the human condition, there would not be sickness.

You have your doctors. They know the conditions within the body when it goes off, and they know the corrections for it. Yet you have a spiritual doctor you never talk to — ever. But you're going to find that out now that you're going to need to know who that one is.

Whatever you call that one — him, her, it — it doesn't matter. It's the presence that heals all things, and the sickness knows that it will be eliminated in the presence of this one. And the human condition, being as it is, enjoys sickness at times because it gets attention from other beings. It's something to complain about, talk about; otherwise, you have nothing to talk about. You don't know what you're talking about, really.

You need to understand the concept of the ability to provide for self in a pleasant manner. Yet you're learning. You're learning. You don't need everything; you need a little bit so that you continue with a little bit and learn, because if you figured you had to carry it up a mountain, you're going to have to leave something on the steps behind, or you'll never get to the top. So each step you take up the mountain, you need to leave something behind because it gets too heavy. Yet when you accept the understanding of descension, everything you have is pleasant for a purpose, for those coming for you to receive, and you don't have to climb the mountain. The mountain comes down to you.

That's the humor within the turtle, the wisdom of the turtle. That's what the shell of the turtle represents: The mountain came down to the being and protected it [the turtle]. And it swims freely in the oceans. God's path is through the oceans, the water. Your planet Earth has been represented as a turtle, eh — the environment, the continents — for a reason, for a reason. Peace to all beings. We are through.

CHAPTER

3

The Supernatural Is Becoming Natural

July 22, 2015

Now [laughs].

What's funny? Humans? [Laughs].

Your words. "Supernatural," what is that? Supernatural like the Virgin Mother's lips moving on that statue? [See figure 2.] That's supernatural?

Figure 2. Virgin Mother statue

Yeah.

That's natural. That's natural. The innocence is in the space. It enjoys participating in a safe manner, sacred manner, with itself and others without necessarily being influenced by others. So supernatural is natural, and that's the secret science of God, we'll call it. This is what the angel Cassiel helps you understand. This symbol here, see this? [See figure 3.]

Oh yes, it is like a glass with six lines in it, diagonals.

That's you.

That's a human?

That's the construct of the subconscious within the skeletal system. That's why it knows where it came from, and it knows where it's going. You are all connected to this concept called God, which is the God within you, that part. Yet the process of supernatural becoming natural is where you are getting caught up.

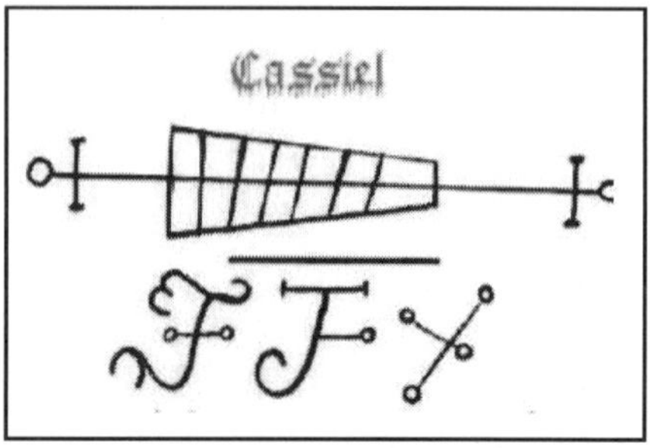

Figure 3. Cassiel Symbols

In between, you're in a natural process, you say. You get up, you walk, you eat, you go to the bathroom, you go to bed, and you sleep. That's natural. It is a part of you that keeps your heart beating when you're sleeping, and you have no idea about it. That's the supernatural connection you have.

The fact that your heart beats when you are not applying any focus on it is an understanding you are not aware of yet. When you can get into that conscious acknowledgment of it — one, two, three, four; one, two, three, four — the beat of the heart, conscious acknowledgment daily, hourly, continually, you will understand supernatural becoming natural because that is how you exist, with breath and water. You have let your minds become convoluted. In your teaching modes, evolution theory — the fishes come out of the water, and there is this evolution thing. But you came out of the water as a fetus. You came out of water as a fetus. You came out of water and breathed and became more with the ingestion of your proper foods and the sustaining of it by the supernatural, if you paid attention.

Now, you're under contracts, but you're not aware of it. You would term them agreements. You'll say you will do something, and it's going to get done because words were used and consciousness was used, and it formed a condition. Those agreements are locked into your astrological chart so that you don't forget inwardly and you maintain a knowledge base of experience. Now, what you are going to find out — and we need to say this as carefully as possible because of the way humans interpret things — you can find it out in one of two ways: (1) You can die the body. Then leave and go in front of your accusers, which are the planetary spiritual forces in your astrological chart. They know what you did, and they know what you did not do. (2) You can understand yourself in the physical reincarnation of trying to improve and correct yourself. Now, listen to the planetary forces of your astrological chart, the spiritual forces, and pay attention to the understanding within you — of what it feels like and what you say when the feelings are not appropriate in the loving condition. You have the ability to alter the consciousness of yourself in regard to previous agreements that you are not aware of yet if you want to start with a clean slate down here. So you adjust and petition.

That's why beings talk to the Moon. That's why you talk to the Sun, because the Moon rules the waters in your consciousness. Actually, the water moves the Moon. You are in that class now. You have seen images of Shiva with the Moon above his head. You have water in your body, 60 to 70 percent water. So that condition in your form (in your body and much of the invisible part of you) runs in here all the time and communicates with that lunar structure.

Accept the Healing of Self for the Healing of Others

Right now, the monks have been told to "monk it." That means, "Do what the monks have been trained to do." That's why you are seeing a lot of the Dalai Lama and these beings moving around the planet to balance energies — because they know how to do it, and it balances it within the crowd. It's a comfort thing going on there. You have this self-identity, and people like to call it an ego, but it's not because you don't even have the ability to think correctly. You don't even know where your thoughts come from, and you don't know who gave you that thought in the first place. Number one, most of your thoughts and information and emotional frequencies are coming from your television and radio frequencies and everybody else's chitchat instead of listening to the Spirit of the Space that's in the invisible. It's between you and the tree. That allows you to be healthy. You don't listen like that anymore. The human condition does not; it is always looking for someone else who knows something more than itself instead of breathing correctly.

One of the things with mantras is to keep the focus in the mind — that's all — so that you can understand yourself and so the bones can appreciate the sinew and appreciate the muscles, because without them the bones can't move. Without your bones, you can't be vertical. You're a puddle. So have appreciation of all of the systems within the body — the heart. The mind is not in the body, what you would say is the mind. You have the brain there, which is your interpreter.

The correct way to interpret, now, is to come down into the solar plexus and the feeling of the self, and then you have a choice: to participate in the energy in "that" direction or participate in the energy in "this" direction. One side of you is black, and one side of you is white. The middle side of you does not know which side is doing what. You need to blend them together. That's the invisible part of you that's symbolized in the tarot card of a little black being with the club and another white being with something else in his hand, a flower [see figure 4]. You've seen it? And everyone's there. You have them both. The wisdom one is the third one that unifies these two. And that's the symbolism of this in the tantric tradition and, what you term, heavy-duty meditation.

Figure 4. The lovers tarot card, Thoth deck

We know you sit like this to receive, to understand, because it is coming here. You are unifying your self. You're pulling the power from one and unifying them together, and then the solid structure (we'll call it the solid structure, the vertebrae) is your tube of consciousness. That's why it's where it is; your elevator shafts, so to speak. You go up and down it here. Most are working from the root up.

Eventually, you move up from the root and settle in the solar plexus. Then from the solar plexus, you start working your way up. You will be breathing consciousness in. You will be accepting, what is termed, the healing of self for the healing of others, not just so that you can be healed. You need to be [healed] because if you're not, you can't help everyone else. You have your agonies, your issues, your things, and your complaints, and this and that and the other. You're there on your back. You just lie down on the cart and can't do anything. You hope you have a bucket.

Well, that portion you're going through now. The human condition is going through the confusion of it. You're going through it. You're going through it. Now you need to do the stabilization process.

Find the Prayer That Matches Your Life

Peace to all beings above. Peace to all beings down below. That'll stabilize the two from interfering with you. Those above you, there, are who interfere with you. Those below you, there, are who interfere with you. Peace to all beings to the left. Peace to all beings to the right. Peace to all beings forward. Peace to all beings in back. Now you have space. Anything comes into that arena you are at, in the present moment when you say, "Peace to all beings," you are expecting it to be peace for all beings. So you are aware. But there will be others who come gently to the edge, and you can sense they're not peaceful. So you say, "Peace to all beings," and put them back. What you use is your dark side for that, to push them back.

"Peace to all beings" sets up the conditions of your perimeter. The more you use it, the more the beings who come into your perimeter will be peaceful. They will feel it, so you're training the inner abilities of your magnetic and electrical current. Now, you are aware of what magnets do. Magnets have an influence on electricity. The left side is your electrical current; the right side is your magnetic current. You are working them both.

Now, electricity moves very rapidly through water. There is not a lot of resistance. When you're working in the spiritual forces for determination and balance, it would be required, necessarily, to have some brass because brass has copper and also has a composition of zinc — 20 percent zinc, something like that — which has resistance to electrical force. It doesn't spark, which is what you're going to need to be aware of because as the atmosphere and you change, you are going to start shooting sparks. You are going to sparkle. But you won't be able to control it. It is already starting to come out of fingers and feet. You need to think of brass, which gets you to the consciousness of the elements zinc and copper. There are colors there, and the merging of those colors is important.

Now we are going to take this back further. Before color, there is a sound, and before sound, there is an intent. What we are trying to do — we, us — through this being is to get you aware of your intent, your intent before the sound of you, before the color of you, and before the manifestation of you, through (what you term) the dispensation of time. Everybody is under the concept that time is one, but that's fine. You're enjoying this lifetime. What did you do in the others? Yes, it's all one. You don't remember the others. You don't have a clue. You're stuck in this one.

So we're going to need to understand self-intent, and that has to take you back before the first memory you have. You will find out it wasn't your intent. It was a pleasurable gift given to you freely with full knowledge of everything and the ability to do whatever. You have total manifestation abilities. In the hand, or however you wanted it, was not a problem. You're going to find what influenced you not to have that, what controlled you out of your pristine, powerful consciousness.

That's what's happening now on your planet. That's why the beings now are communicating with extraterrestrials. It's not about extraterrestrials. It is not about extraterrestrials. It is about a prayer. I said "a prayer." Pick one, and your life, that is what it is about. Now, you can't get any simpler than that. I can't get any simpler than that. You need to find the prayer that matches your life.

Now, if Master Jesus has taught other teachers and has been said to be their teacher by them, he gave the prayer. I don't know how to express it anymore. We have already told you it is a compilation of his experiences as David through 150 psalms living in the presence of the I Am-ness of the invisible one, we'll say. So he reduced it for simple beings. The disciples, they were not that smart. They were not that smart. Peter was called "ye of little faith." He's the founder of a church of little faith, basically. Your current pope realizes that, and he knows who the instigator and antagonist are. But people don't like to hear that because they are associated with that being; that's why. They are becoming frustrated with the pope's messages now, particularly in your country, here.

Now you're in a quandary, and you have no one to pay attention to anymore. You don't. You have channels here, channels there, same thing going on, same thing. So that's why we've said pick a prayer. Use it daily. All you have to do is say two words, "Our Father." That's it. Or say deep within the sigh, "God." It doesn't have to have a name. The answer comes if you are open and understanding. It is a vertical thing from the heart chakra–solar plexus. It goes straight up. It is total surrender. It is like using the tarot cards with beings [coming] out of their coffins with their hands up, like that [see figure 1]. That's it. You surrendered to that, that great and glorious light there. That's Gabriel, in that particular form, with the horn. The sound of the horn is awakening within the self.

The Intent Is in the Sound and the Beat of Your Heart

The conditions now on your planet are set, so no one has to die unless he or she wants to. You have a cloud, a wave of a death wish, coming over the East Coast, a wave of despondency coming over the West Coast, in the astral. People are being affected by it. They don't want to be here. You want to be someone else. They don't understand — complain, complain, complain, complain. Pray! That's what prayers are for. That's what the masters have been saying. That's what mantras are for, actually — mantras, or what you would term, "Well, this is how I want to do it. I don't want to pray that one. I will do this." Good, fine, you'll find the intent later.

It's difficult to get true teaching here so that the application can be understood. Why? There are too many words. The intent is in the sound and the beat of your heart. It's there — I be … I be … I be … I be — four chambers, four beats, four letters in the holy name [IHOH], simple understanding. Then you're going to find out, basically, "I am yours, father. Do with me as you wish." That's the way it is. Then you'll find out as that's done, it is to help someone else to stand on his or her own feet. It's not to follow anyone. You have enough gurus. You are all gurus. Well, start "guruing" it!

You can't. You can't because you haven't studied what you call the interior self. The interior self, the fearful self, the self that is dying daily in the inside you — inside everyone — it is happening with everyone. It's a pitiful crying thing asking for mercy, in a way, for the ignorance within the system.

Now, as you begin to work with the invisible forces as they enter the body, you make a condition, "If you come into my body, could you clean it up a little bit? That would be appropriate for you because I have not the awareness inside yet for how to do that." Just a little bit. You don't want a dramatic clearing because you might be bouncing around on the floor for a while. You want just a little gentle clearing. So the agreement is you're amenable to them working through you and with you. They're amenable so that they can help clean you up a little bit. Then you adjust and start cleaning yourself up, and you begin to interact with these beings through you, "Oh yes, I understand." They're not here to intimidate. They are here to teach and assist in the continuity of life, no matter where you are or when you are. That's what's happening now. That's what's happening now.

You are getting so much force upon the planet, and within the consciousness of the human condition, people need to be recognized. That is why everyone is starting to stand up and say something. But you need to be recognized within the self. Who is recognizing you? It is the Invisible One That Is. There is a runaway process that starts thinking things over. "Who is that thinking?" Breathe. Be thankful for the water in the body. Be thankful for the oracle who receives the depleted oxygenated blood and the ventricle that pumps it and pushes it back out. There is a being in there.

Your heart was made from the same material as your bones. It just took a different path and became a different entity. It shifted, same thing with all your organs. It came from the same seed and the same unification with the egg. You knew how to do it because you let it alone, and the invisible force built it for you because you didn't know how you did it. You come out with appreciation of form, but you forgot who formed you, how the thought of you formed you before the union of the mother and father. Then the mother and father help condition the image in the construct you call this system because you're much more than this. You actually find yourself in the space between the stars and as stars. As a star, at times, it becomes boring out there. You're just standing, shining. You want to do something. This is what you're doing.

The holographic image of your celestial kingdom, your star systems, the imaging force, is in the bone of the skull. The North Star stays where it is, and everything else goes around it. It's starting to activate. The North Star is the gate of Tarsus. It's where Uriel stands. Beings are getting ready to approach that gate. Now, whether you go through it or not is a different story. There is a crowd of angels around there. In front and before and two big ones by the door and their wings definitely have definition to them. They don't go out sideways. They go up and come down with authority. That door is about ready to open, and there will be ones who go through to understand the experience of All That Is and come back through to share that experience.

There will be ones who sit and hold it, so the door stays open, for a while anyway. This is the experience you're getting ready for. It's coming faster than we thought, because when pictures mouth, there's a connection there, and there will be many, many, many, many, many to disprove it. Since it is real, they can't influence that, and that frightens them. You're going to start seeing statues move, and when statues move, you stay still. Go sacred and think of something besides your self, because there is something else moving that statue. This one [the channel] has seen them; that happened. It is a cautionary understanding in that. There is much more to the space between you and the tree than you think there is. And it's not the being that you understand as, what you say, gnomes, elementals. It's much more than that. They all recognize this one. That's where they came from. They know what it's for. You're in that (how you say?) force field now.

Can you say who the force field is?

Part of the invisibleness. The twinkling in the air is what you knew before Atlantis and before bodies were physical. That's what you knew. Then the becoming of the body — the becoming of the human condition — there was a limitation of the ability to respond and think in an appropriate manner. Forgetfulness came upon self, and that was where the ego was developed. You learned separateness, so you had to identify yourself as separate. You forgot how you were not separate yet unified but angry. That created more separateness, and that's what's going on.

You're an animal consciousness — tiger, bear, fish, monkey, ape, gorilla, giraffe — but you don't know it. That's where you got your idea of movement of life, from the animal kingdom. The human condition resembles the ambulatory nature of the apes and monkeys with the thumbs. That's where you got your idea. The invisible portion … you saw the experience of these entities, but you didn't want to become one of them. You wanted to become different with the application of their force or how they learned to use that force.

ETs: This Is Not Their Planet

When you're getting involved with these extraterrestrials, which is beginning to happen more and more, you're forgetting yourself. This is not their planet. You shouldn't invite beings here unless you know them. The thing to do with the experience with the extraterrestrials is set up a conference before when you go to sleep and visit them in your sleep state. Then learn to be and work and understand, if it is appropriate. But you're going to find out that it isn't because you are very isolated for a reason, for a reason.

A lot of the systems within the extraterrestrial condition bred the soul out of the body, and now they're trying to get it back. They don't have feelings. They can't understand feelings. Feelings are the compassion and mercy of God or what you use to develop it. As you are in God school, you're going to learn something for the application of others, not the selfish application of self. In one way, being more selfish is becoming more God-ish, yet you'll be alone. Selfishness is the understanding of, what you call, perpetuosity, and the innocence of you is a different understanding. That means you don't want to be influenced by someone you don't want to be influenced by.

Hopefully soon, people are going to be able to choose, select willingly, to be with ones whose understanding is wiser, and usually that means the space is quiet because your body is a temple. As you understand the "templeness" of your body and the spiritual beings coming to help clean it up, you become more profound. You find you have a candle "here," a candle "there," a candle in your hips, a candle in your stomach, a candle at your crown, a candle at your knees, a candle at the elbows, and a candle at your ankles. Little flames of fire that keep you in the understanding of you, of your sacredness. You're a walking temple.

Yet the human condition, the ego you say, does not appreciate the fact that it is a temple. It is a temple mainly because of the confusion within the systems you call the churches and the controlling aspects of that over everyone else. Instead of developing the consciousness as a temple idea within each one so that they can understand the safety of themselves, wherever they are in the presence, you start moving in different arenas; you affect people by just being there.

The crystalline structure of your bones now is changing to a higher frequency. It's becoming more white, more light, and more electrical. Like in the Indiana Jones movies, these beings in the crystal skull, they just go "bzzz" [makes vibrating sound], like that. You are becoming that.

You Will Still Be You

Now, one of the reasons the struggle is so hard in the working condition in your world now is this word "penance." You beings are going through your penance. You've done it enough. Now it's time to claim your power, and you call for the manifestations. The next phases in the human condition are those, and Sai Baba taught it is the manifestation and ability in the hand. When you understand the requirement, you understand the ease of it. It's not a necessity that you manifest in your hand; it's a process known. It's not done by you. It's done for you, actually. When you get that understanding, you have conquered what we would term the invisibility of space, because you are working with the invisibles within the space now. That's the next level. That's the next level. It's a whole different level of appreciation. That's why we use health to the body, mind, and spirit in the center of your temple. "Peace to all beings" is your perimeter. Health to the body, mind, and spirit. Then when you get health to the body, mind, and spirit, you add strength to body, mind, and spirit.

You call it strength, which comes from your planet, strength of the planet, which comes up. Then you will have the integrity to come down and understand what it is and then work with it. This is the process, which is occurring within the human condition now. Everyone's going through it. July is a particularly interesting month, and you have one more week with it. Then you're going into, what we will say, a kite ride in the air of August.

The invisibles are beginning to make themselves known. The process of coming from physical manifestation and darkness out of the cave to the invisible light, which is visible light when it wants to be, is a process that you're going through now. Everyone is. Everyone is. You're basically going through the discussion, everyone is with themselves, about what they don't like with themselves because you're seeing it reflected out in front of you. So the adjustments and frequencies are what are occurring. That's what happens when these beings hear the sound in the sky, and there's no one playing music over loudspeakers. There is an adjustment in consciousness going on, gently at times, gently, gently, gently, because the ability for the human condition to go crazy is exceptionally well known.

The mind and the brain cannot function at certain speeds.

There will be a tendency to just say blah, blah, blah, say with no control. We are working to establish that ability to control. That means it needs to calm down and sense the space and realize you're going through a process of healing, spiritual healing. Your walking it, you're working, through it. You're going to walk out of it as soon as you drop some pretty severe baggage. That's the process now.

You are going to learn to readjust your thoughts. You're going to find out your thoughts are yours. You're going to find out who is giving you other ones and that their influence is not about you. You are actually going to get another suit of clothes, but you will be you.

CHAPTER

4

The Movement of the Emotional Condition Called Expression

July 28, 2015

There is another level of things we have to bring, and there's another level we have to push so that there can be acceptance of the things to bring. So these are steps in the …

So this book is like a beginning step, then?

Yeah, it's a beginning step so that people can at least think in a particular direction for when the movement, as Isis says, "You are going to be running," and …

If you are around water.

Well, there's a running in consciousness too, because as everyone starts their panic thing, people pick it up. So this particular book creates a basis within the understanding of safety within the self and spirit. The human condition now is getting, literally, a physical introduction to the spiritual forces besides the human self. You're hearing the voices of them from out of the air. You're feeling the presence of them when you get goose bumps, goose bumpy. You are beginning to acknowledge they are familiar with you though you're not as familiar with them as you should be. That is developing, that communal understanding with the spiritual forces from the unseen world and the physical condition. That is the next communal understanding.

Adjust to Your Next Phase of Existence

Now, as we go into … we probably shouldn't use those words "as we go into another phase of existence." As another phase of existence comes to you, you're going to have to adjust to it. This is what's happening. This is the movement of the emotional condition called expression. You are 60 percent to 70 percent water. It depends on the physical point. When you are younger, you have more, and when you are older, you have less.

So it is the consciousness of the water that you're learning to control, and you haven't done well with it. That was the example in the Christian tradition and the Tibetan tradition of beings walking on water. It's the consciousness of the water accepting the being walking on the water. So that has a great control of the emotional consciousness within any construct because water is the emotional understanding in this life. Otherwise, you'd just be a piece of bacon.

The human condition knows how to communicate with the water — not necessarily verbally, but when you're thinking in your normal process of being a normal, average, what you call, human that doesn't study spiritual understanding, there's an inner communication with the water and the self. There is. You know you have to drink it. There's a recognition and thankfulness deep inside, especially if you're dying of thirst, that type of thing. So there is that essence there. Yet the human condition, and because of some other influences that allowed the brain and the thought processes not to be processed appropriately within the physical construction, has you caught in this great trap that you're going to come out of now.

We have said before God's path is through the water. The divine force, name there, this force is moving through the water. It's going to move a lot of things. You have not seen, well, you have, one you have. In your time, you have seen the tsunami in the Japan region. That is a baby tsunami of what is going to occur. You're going to have waves from your Atlantic Ocean reaching your state of Pennsylvania. You're going to have waves from what you call your Pacific Ocean overflooding Oregon, Washington (state), California, and coming to the border of Arizona and through Arizona, actually. Tucson and those areas in your south are not going to be there. They're going to be underwater all the way to the southern part of New Mexico and Texas.

Humankind's consciousness and the abuse of the sacredness of nature herself are going to come to the forefront. No one has been able to sit and communicate with the space, not yet. They are communicating with the entities within the space, and they're communicating with the spiritual forces that are past, the spiritual forces that have not yet become present, and the spiritual forces that have been retrograded. They know they're going to be saved eventually, but they have some making-up things to do.

Nobody understands that the nature of the space is what gives you the grace to perform your functions, and your function is learning. It's called eternity. You keep going and going, and you learn something, and you become greater. You assist more, assist more, and assist more. You find out the reason for the assistance is the blessing in itself. It is a blessing there. This is the process the human condition is in now. Particularly your (how say you?) ...

you're going to be able to think in a vertical condition, walking, like … and as you were the fetus still in your mother's womb. Yet you will be a walking, vertical human in an adult form. The understanding of the fetus yet as you were with your mother in the womb, you had a presence there. You knew you were growing up and establishing a form. You knew it. You are in the same process now. You are in a fetus form. Now, the difficult part here is there becomes a disintegration of consciousness and a disintegration of your physical form within yourself in space and time.

You have three anchors. Space is one. Time is another, and the self, now, in your frequency adjustments, which occurs in the sternum at the solar plexus and moves to the heart chakra, that's your big tambourine, basically. When that vibrates at a certain frequency, you move into a transparent mode. That transparent mode is when your abilities pass your hands through tables and things start taking place. You move into transparent. You will see yourself becoming transparent; your hand will become invisible. You will be seeing more space. You will be looking through your hand, and you will see the tree, first off. Then you will see the transparency of your natural force. Then you will understand the purpose for the flesh and the bones, the sacredness of the bones and why your name is so important to those bones, because that is what holds you.

Humans don't understand that yet. In a manner of the blessing that occurs within the bones, manufactured, is your blood. That's where it comes from. That's where it comes from, and you have forgotten that by listening to others. So you're going through this phase of purification with your own divine influence within the form called the self body with the self called spirit. Togetherness is the unification of the presence of knowledge. You are displaying your knowledge of what you know in body form right now. That's it, nothing more.

As you breathe easier, you begin to breathe a thought. You don't think a thought; that's old school. You breathe the thought and have the patience to witness the manifestation of it. Then your timing within the space becomes justified within yourself. You do it again and the timing shrinks; manifestation happens faster, faster, faster. Then you are in your knowledge place system, yourself, and then pretty soon like-mannered-based systems come together, and the construct becomes pretty dramatic.

You create safety zones and color because that is the first emphasis of sound manifested visually. You learn to work appropriately with the colors of self, not as it has been in the past to influence others and control, but into the understanding that everyone deserves health. Everyone deserves a presence in the space. as its been determined to be that, there they are now, and everyone deserves the comfort of peace in that space — peace, protection, and joy within that space.

You learn how space is utilized for grace in the understanding of your own spiritual force, which is basically the name of freedom. Everyone's spiritual force, basically ... its name is freedom. It was determined that way. That's the essence of your own knowledge. You are a free being. Complexity comes in and the fear of safety of self, so at this timing in your planetary system, we're taking you through that, assisting you through that fear consciousness of the single unity of self without other entities for companionship. You're going through that now. Pretty soon everyone is going to understand what they are doing a little bit, at least some, and there will be a collective ability to move space so everyone is adjusted in the teachings in an appropriate manner, sitting in their space if they're supposed to be moving or whatever.

Be Thankful for the Breath

Space is shifting. The space itself is shifting, which means your time of grace is coming to a close. The water is going to cause this understanding to come forward because when you realize that you have very powerful emotional content within each one, then you can stabilize the space. You asked permission for the space to be granted its, what you call, cubic structure at this time and then its conical structure. Right now, you're cubic. So you need those directions, six directions — above, below, north, south, east, and west.

In the stabilization of your magnetic currents here, now, we have to add an additional equation. The magnetic influence of your poles affects your brain. The ability for the synapses to have visions, to see beyond beyond, to have these experiences as, we'll say, ones have had with your LSD-type things, it's a magnetic influence. As your pole energy starts shifting, this magnetic influence is going to increase in the left hemisphere and the right hemisphere of the brain. Each hemisphere reacts differently, and it presents a portion with pictures. Some come up with the demonic stuff, symbols and things and beings, as real and others not. Yet the understanding there … and then those images go away. You understand that they are images; you will understand that they are images in the preparation for self-sanctity of self; that's it.

The human condition is going through its knowledge of its own death process right now while you're walking. As a matter of fact, you're having your past-life reviews right now as you are walking because you are thinking back on things. This is consciousness understanding. Your movies have presented these things for you, so perhaps that's the condition, but it is, and you're going through it now. You're going through past-life reviews. So once you understand this in the *Pamphlet for Life*, every moment is a past-life review, yet every moment is a new moment and what you call the presence and the presentation of life anew.

You don't have to keep looking backward anymore. You should have the wisdom of it. So you look forward, and then you become a different form of breathing. What will happen is there will be a breath that comes out of your solar plexus, literally. It will come out in front of you. It will go up into your nostrils. You breathe it in and let it go down. You will find the self of you inside you wants to breathe you because, as we talked about earlier, let this other being breathe you. It's the self that's different from the body, but it is within the body. It knows how to breathe. So the first junction of this, we're going to call this the magic elixir, only it's the breath of air released from the solar plexus that comes up into the nostrils. You breathe it in [inhales] and down back to the solar plexus, and that will acknowledge the being there.

Then the heart starts getting registrations for you, say, and the heart chakra starts getting its clearances for the seals there that'll come. You see in the seals there in Tibetan symbolism things with the chakras. Those are there, and once you get them locked on, then the breath within begins to understand it's appropriate — the occurrences of the throat chakra, occurrences of the sixth seal, and those things. Once the throat chakra opens, those are commands. That's a command. When the throat opens from here, things will get done because that's the overlord of the particular space you are in there.

You're working with a force that's much larger than yourself. It's huge, we'll say. It can't get all of itself into your body. It can't. It has tried in the human condition, and it can't. It's too much powerful knowledge for the limitations held within the constructs here. You beings don't talk to the inner parts of yourselves, so if this force came in, there'd be disconcertment. There'd be antagonism. It'd be unhealthy at first because of the argument of the body not willing to stretch itself. You would feel goose bumps and things, but that's just on the surface. It comes and wants to stretch. It stretches and pushes out things. You almost feel as if you're going to blow up like a balloon and burst.

But — this is tricky — the knowledge is the movement your lymphatic system assists in your ability to regulate this thing in the manner of an, as you say, accelerator and a decelerator. You learn how to slide your lymphatic nodules, we'll say. It's not really a nodule. It's a … not a shut off switch; it's a slide that allows a certain amount of fluid to flow, and then it shuts it off. It doesn't completely shut it off, and there's an intellectual understanding in there. It protects the most sensitive portions of the inner self, which is getting down to the soul's level, which is what's occurring now.

This force is going to make statues and move statues. So if a statue is there beside you and it starts to move you, you start standing like a statue. Then there's a reciprocity there, and it balances. So that's what's going to happen.

What we're trying to do is to get the teachings to the human condition of the thought of thankfulness each moment for each breath and thankfulness along the same time for the space to be able to breathe within it because then you can think or have a process and moment of self. So thankfulness for the breath and the space, and then of course you will come to the thankfulness for the water and your foods. But generally, first off, you need to be thankful for the breath and the ability in the thoughts that come and the space. That's why all the old prophets would hide in caves. They wouldn't be influenced by others because in one way — you haven't learned this yet — but you drag space with you when you move from one place to another place. You bring the thoughts of the space and the items of the space in "this and that," and you keep thinking of the space. So you are dragging space with you, but you don't realize it. You think they're just things.

As space shifts, so does your cubic understanding. You become more fluidic. You become more like a bird, understanding the wind and being pushed by the wind and understanding who flies you, at times, because the bird knows it's not the only one flying it. The animal knows it's not the only one walking it. The animal knows its not just walking itself. There are other beings and other systems there. The human condition is in this meeting place between the true aspects of nature, the animals and the beings you can't see who talk to the animals and work with them, and the human condition acknowledging the animals and the beings who are talking to the animals and the usefulness of all of it for the human condition.

The Process Called Life

With a pleasant understanding, not with this, in a manner I'll say, many have thought to conquer the world, old ones, conquer all of them. You can't. You can't, unless you are big enough to walk around it in one day. You can't do it. The spatial reference there is to the, we're going to call it, ignorance of the fall. In the human condition, everyone thought they were going to, at one level, come into this place and have a grand old time and do what they wanted to do, but it didn't happen that way. But you knew about it. Before birth, you were anticipating it, but it didn't happen. Now you're meeting the adjudicator that set it up so that it didn't happen and is training you for another purpose, for another purpose. That purpose is to be a guardian of space for others to learn within, basically. That's your job now.

Your place in positions of consciousness where you have a feeling more than others would have a feeling for awareness is … there are some humans who are going to start establishing verbal contact and visual contact with the spiritual forces that are around all over and working together daily, hourly, uniquely, innocently, creating safety for others. That is going to be the main thing right now, creating safety in space for others, because it's going to be traumatic. This is the process of the evolution of worlds. That's why you have the bodhisattvas. They came back. They didn't have to. They could've gone on, but they understood the uniqueness and the beauty within the human condition, and they offered to assist. They are now; they're assisting everyone who will pay attention.

There are guardians of those who even aren't paying attention but want to assist you. By "assist," I mean more for protection and blessings because you only learn when you do something, even when you make a mistake. You know it was a mistake. You correct it and do it again, and then eventually you get it. You try one thing once, and it didn't work. You try it twice, you try it three times, and a little improvement there, and then the improvement becomes yourself. You have improved yourself. You know it. It looks like an external process, but then you understand it is an internal process. Why? Because you did it! Even though others said things, you're in the process of living it. You are the doer of it.

Each individual is the doer of his or her own destiny and the preciseness of, what you call, the capacity to be of service to others who are not aware of the sacred nature of space. It's service oriented, and those who are not of service will not be around much longer, you're going to find.

The Presence, with a capital P, the Holy Presence, with a capital HP, is always in the space. It might not entertain you, and by that, I mean watch you as you're doing your mischief and things, but it is always there and aware of it. It is time now for the human condition to always be aware of that Holy Presence being there, and then you will feel the influence of it. It won't make you any greater than any other. It will simply keep you safer and healthier. That's what it will do. That's why it's offering the simple words "health to the body, mind, and spirit" and the contemplation of that causes a residence in there. It's a command. The bones resonate that command — health to the body, mind, and spirit — and it tries to adjudicate that within the process of your movement. In other words, keep you out of places that might be not comfortable for you. That's why you have this opportunity now to forget things. "I was going in this direction, but it didn't ..." What happened? It changed. Health to body, mind, and spirit is doing that.

Okay, let's see what we have now. "Peace to all beings" is a concept you need to understand when you're in communication with others because if you don't have peace to all beings surrounding you, then the conflicts will start and the arguments. Peace to all beings and then you can have conversation, or there will be more of an authoritative flavor coming through. So these are simple little steps in being ... you're going to find soon there will be more ceremonies going on — little circle group "here," little circle "there," little circle "there" — each doing their own. Yet they'll be linking up "here," up "here," and then it spreads and spreads and spreads.

You're going to have a communal understanding on the planet, eventually, instead of this separation process that you're going through. This is the process, and the communal understanding that frightens everyone because you saw what happened with your religious churches. There's a communal understanding there. But it became a control thing over everybody — not as sharing or caring. Some do little, but the great church is going to call that coming as going to teach everyone the same lesson. You're breathing the same air, and you're drinking the water. Careful. I'm in it. You're going to feel that being as it expresses itself and creates dizziness in the mind. You literally could fall down from dizziness because as you approach the greaterness, you have no thought; you have no ability to think. You're a receiver at that point. This is the Presence as it manifests. That's what's working within this, what you call, Pamphlet for Life, which starts as the outer layer of your flesh, your skin, rather, which is your breathing apparatus for your flesh, which is a sensitive tool — sensitive tool — to understand the knowledge and density supported by the sinew and the muscle and the bone so that you can move about and rescue yourself if you need to. But it's mainly for the flesh purpose, the flesh. It's a really soft, sensitive thing in there.

Before the flesh, you were light, and the flesh manifested out of the colors of the rainbows. You picked one from the sound. The skin is your breathing apparatus, really. You beings get caught up in the color of it. What's important is the tone within the bones. Your colors change because you pretty much look like chameleons (most of the time, anyway) shifting color patterns. But you don't for safety reasons, we'll say. The other thing that happens is when you go through this little process now, you're going to begin to find you've been caught in a trap, an old one, an old one, old trap. You've heard the story, but you didn't believe it. That's what the recognition is coming for, the identification and the purification of the self — the pure being of you, the divine one that goes back for a long, long way, beyond even the concept of, what you would term, time.

So the Pamphlet for Life is your self. You are that. It starts with the bones and your tone, your breath, and the understanding of what thought is; that is not you yet. You beings use your beads and some religions use, what you say, the rosary. The Tibetans have their beads, and other systems have their beads for the continuity of the consciousness and prayers. Your spinal columns are your walking beads. If you started at your pelvis and moved up daily, considering each bone, you can pray your beads this way. As you walk, your bones in your vertebrae are doing the prayers for you. You just need to understand that it's coming down through the crown chakra. As you stand vertically, it'll come down to the pelvis, and the bones will be acknowledging prayers.

You will walk differently, you will talk differently, you will see differently, you will hear differently, and you'll be experiencing the Presence of the space differently because everything within it will begin to acknowledge you. That's the process. There are some in the human condition doing it now in your Tibetan culture. There are beings we call the walkers. They walk to stabilize space. This is the condition the humans were designed for. So this is what you're going through physically in the body, the process called life.

The Self Is Going to Solve the Problem

Now, okay we are through unless you have something you want to communicate about.

I do have a question I'm very concerned about. Can the human condition change? You said water would cover all these states. That's a prediction. Can we change it? Can we protect those people?

There are warnings starting to be given, and if they pay attention, they can. Prayers will shift the current, actually, to the South Atlantic hitting the East Coast; prayers will descend the energy to the south and avert this. But the way the human condition works is sometimes they need a big smack to really get it. We're, how you say, pulling strings to slow it down, to modify it in a way, so that it's not as dramatic as proposed, as others are. Prayers will help. But that's the only thing that's going to help. You're in a shift. Everybody's going through this disbelief. "That can't happen," and when it happens, it's been told. But this is where the structure of prayer will really come forth because you will see Space stopping this. Space itself will stop it.

Can you give me the words of a prayer the people who will read this can say?

Well, you must know this one, "Om Mani Padme Hum" and right after that, "Om Tat Sat." It balances. "Om Mani Padme Hum, Om Mani Padme Hum, Om Tat Sat." They become commands. The bones start talking, and then things happen.

Okay. That's one. Is there something that people who aren't familiar with ... ?

In the Christian tradition?

Not necessarily Christian, but people who don't feel connected to the "Om Mani Padme Hum."

Okay. I'm going to use this word. It refers to the Great Spirit, but the word is "Father," and then it's "have mercy." And it's going to take a union, a male entity, saying, "Father, have mercy," and a female entity saying, "Mother, have mercy" together. That's going to slow it down together.

Is there an estimated date for this to happen? No earlier than or no later than or something?

I'll put it this way: You are going to start seeing the warning signs. Well, you're already seeing the warning signs. You have volcanoes going off all over the place and the earthquakes. Japan just had another three 7.0s yesterday, something like that, and it's starting to go around the Ring of Fire, and Alaska had another seven yesterday also, three or four of them. You're going to feel it. So your awareness is not there, and knowing it's coming, you don't know what to do. But you can see the situation. If you said to a Californian, "You're going to have a 10.0 earthquake, and there are tsunamis that are going to go to Arizona; you'd better move," they're not going to move. They will wait until the tsunami comes, and they'll say, "I should've moved." They have children in school, they have houses, they have "this" and "that," and they have to go see the movies. They are not interested until it's too late. So the warning signs are building.

I will say, just for this information, September is going to be very interesting, *really* interesting. The majority of humans haven't built up a prayer wall, and they haven't said prayers to establish these conditions in "this" part and establish the conditions in "this" part, establish the conditions "here." They haven't. They don't even know what it is. And you really don't have issues with this, even talking about it. You have your religion over "here" and your religion over "there" and your religion over "there." "This" religion is killing "this" religion. That doesn't make any sense to anybody in any form of enlightenment. So you're seeing it in front of you. This is all a process to bring forth the one that's going to solve the problem. Well, the one that is going to solve the problem is not going to be the one that's really going to solve the problem.

The individual entity (called the self) incorporated within the human condition (called the bones and the flesh) is going to solve the problem because it is going to decide it doesn't want to be involved in the problem anymore. That's what's going to happen because you are all equal power. You're all the same. As the shifting occurs, you will notice it. You can check out your earthquakes and your earthquake lists and be put on a list to be notified and also with volcanoes. You have more volcanoes going off than have gone off ever. There's ones, three or four a day. We have this vehicle [Arthur] watching three or four a day going off, new ones in regions that have been dormant for a long time. So the movement of this great sphere is beginning to happen, literally.

Gaia, she is moving and venting, venting, venting. Lava is not something to mess with. It consumes. Fire, that's all it does is just consume, consume, consume. This is what creates new lands and new species. You're seeing the results of the Fukushima accident. The flowers over there are not growing correctly. They're mutant. The fish, you're losing in the sea. The radiation has already reached your beaches in your California, Oregon, and Washington states, but they're not telling anybody. You're poisoning yourself and your mother — your caretaker while you're from the spiritual world incorporated here. Your mother has a responsibility to protect that incorporation in a greater sense, and she's going to do it for those, as you would understand, who she found worthy for continuance. That's part of that process now. Spiritual understanding in the human condition world is not there, not yet.

Spiritual understanding is really the appreciation and awareness of all life, the appreciation of it. You can see it, another being there, other entities, beings, different animals. You're not alone because if they weren't there, you would be alone, alone. You wouldn't know not to eat the rocks; you wouldn't know what to do. So you're not alone, and you're in a precious experience of the self developing. That's what's really happening for all eternity — growing, whatever.

You're being prepared. In one manner of understanding, if you really knew what was going on, you are being coddled step by step to go through this, because this experience, what is occurring on your planet now, hasn't happened before. It hasn't. You've had wars before. For centuries, you've had wars. For thousands and thousands of years, you have had countries trying to conquer countries and beings trying to conquer. But this one you have not experienced before. No.

The owner of the planet is going to show up. Those are *my* words. People can attribute it to what they want to attribute it. I probably should say the owner of all the planets, the one that gave you the authority to have an astrological chart working with the spiritual forces of the planets that surround this place, which is your birth date. Humans don't understand that yet, the authority they're given there. They think they are at the mercy of this force, but you sat there and agreed and talked over it before you were born so that you could accomplish something within self. That is always the way it is. So self can learn, no matter where it is — another animal, preferably. You would choose human again, as you understand yourselves, or a little higher frequency in a spiritual form that can transition in and out like Shiva does at times, or any of those beings. Bodhisattvas do it too. But you're in that training because there's privileges granted there. One of the privileges is overcoming this fear of death thing. Overcoming all fears, that's the privilege of working in this condition now — gained when completed, okay.

Thank you. Where is the water coming from? Up from within the center of the planet?

Well, your state has a seven-mile-wide river underneath it that runs from north to south. It is partially going to come up from there.

Then there will be a condition, which is … you know how you have clouds and they rain?

Mm-hmm.

No clouds, no clouds, no clouds, just an explosion of water from clear air. It will frighten people, will look like waterfalls.

Then also from the oceans onto the shores … ?

Yes. The water here, now, under your state is fresh water, so when that comes up, that's drinking water. That will be available. The saltwater that's coming in through the south will not be drinkable. It is saltwater.

Okay, so we can't get this book out to warn people before this happens, then. I mean, you're saying that there's … I don't want to lose all these states and all these people.

We have a condition. There has been placed in your computer structures and things …

The Internet?

These sounds that are being heard in your Europe over different countries, like trumpets and things in the air there, no band playing, totally unique. They're celestial sounds. They're warning sounds. They have begun to occur in your state called Michigan, celestial sounds. Those are warning sounds. You can see it on your videos and hear it on the videos, people exclaiming, "Oh, what? That's not construction equipment. That's different." They're talking about it. It's going to occur all over. It is celestial sounds. They are warning sounds.

This has been going on in your Europe for over a year, and now it has moved over to your United States. We will call it "moved" because it has to do with the magnetic and electrical shift that's going on that's creating the sounds and the atmosphere. It's not a UFO or ships singing music. It's not that. It is an electrical and magnetic phenomenon making sound. It produces colors, and you all came in this world pattern on a particular color stream. That's the uniqueness of you as it's working. These things are becoming apparent now. They're making some beings look further to what's going on, much further. It's an interior process. You beings have heard this process for so long. "It's inside. It's inside. It's inside." The knowledge comes from the inside depth of self because you already know this in one way.

You are at a place where you are finding out the worth of your prayers, really, how strong you are there, how strong you are in that, because that's what changes the space. I can't make that any clearer, but maybe I should use another word for prayer. Your petitions for safety for others, that's different. I guess it's the same. But it's still the same, as it takes intensity to get it there, to get the answer and correction from it, you see.

For example, in your biblical text, David went through a lot of suffering — suffered, suffered, suffered, suffered, suffered, suffered, suffered. And Jesus, being David, gave the answer to the suffering, which is the Lord's Prayer — which is for the Lords, by the Lords, from the Lords, to the Lords. If you really understand that, the suffering does not have to take place. But it is not understood. He gave it. He didn't charge a commission for it. He didn't say, "Pay me," every time you have to say it. He gave it because it worked. It's been a while since beings really understood those pauses there. The words have changed. They changed some things because, "Well, I thought it felt better 'this' way." They'll figure it out. But it starts with "Our Father" and the understanding and the balance we have to get here is between the male frequency called Father and the female frequency called Mother.

There's a big distortion going on here in the human condition about that thing. That's what's causing the problems. One's electrical, and one's magnetic. Talk to electricity; you get a different answer. Talk to a magnet; you get a different answer. Maybe that's the condition we should get people to talk to: Talk to electricity first, and then talk to magnets. See if you can get them working together. You'll end up frying yourself. It's a process because you're half-magnetic, and you're half-electrical. Left side's electrical. Right side's magnetic.

You're the duality. That's the image of Shiva being blue and white, and he switches. Shiva did that not to say, "Look how great I look and how beautiful I am." He does demonstrations: "This is the process, and this is how you do it."

Which is which? Blue is electric?

White is the electric. The black is the magnetic. Black is on your right side, which is a tone of blue, actually, when you figure it out, blue, bluish. Well, another thing I'll tell you is that you come from the blue throne, but you don't know that yet. What blue throne? That's my humor. That's what lapis lazuli represents, the gold in it, which is the golden thread of life — which you are from the throne, basically. We'll put it that way, okay.

Thank you. That was quite an answer to my question.

Try to remember the blue throne because that comes out of Sirius, the Sirius system. Well, there's a black hole there. We've taken beings through that before, where the dragon force of thought is, original thought, when it comes through there. You have thoughts that are different in the humans. That's where the blue throne is, of consciousness. You will still be able to think and communicate because for certain levels, your ability to think has to stop because you are not the provider there.

You are making the connection now between Sirius, and that's what is happening with all of these planets going retrograde now. Everything's going retrograde, so you go back through your stuff that you've gone through, and you thought you were going to clear it. So don't be surprised if you repeat the stuff and déjà vu becomes apparent. If déjà vu starts coming up, that means you have been doing this before, and you recognize it. Just step to the left a little bit, or to the right, to change it. You are repeating it because it was not done correctly the first time, not because you were so good that you are doing it again. Okay?

Thank you so much.

Health to the body, mind, and spirit. Peace to all beings. Strength to body, mind, and spirit. Courage for the soul now, where you have this one to come. Courage for the soul. It's time the soul was acknowledged, so courage for the soul. That's what's working the body, mind, and spirit. We are through.

CHAPTER

5

Silver Dragon Energy

August 4, 2015

We are bringing in a new energy today, an introduction both for the being coming and for you meeting the being. This is, we'll say, a descriptive force without a name. It's like silver dragon energy, very metallic, very concerned, concerning the students' understanding of the frequency of themselves becoming. You have to move into your becoming state in order to communicate — you call it communication — with these sorts of frequencies. This is all in the path of life.

You are educating yourself with your breath and those who breathe through you, but you're not aware of that. When you eat your foods, your food are breathing through you. You consider the digestive process as the food giving you energy. That is not the true case. The true case is you are ingesting the breath of the life force that created the breath, that used breath — the breathing of the vegetables, grapes, it doesn't matter; it all breathes. That is what is the true nature of the continuity of your existence. It's the breath within the foods, not the chemicals and not the chemical reactions as you think. Well, the chemical reactions actually are instigators of the breath, but that's another thing.

The process now on your planet of becoming — of working — is breathing correctly. That's all. You have your tantric breaths, your meditation breaths, your swimming breath, you're running breath, and you're sleeping breath. All these other breaths you have, and your food is breathing through you. This concept needs to be understood because then you will appreciate the space that the food is grown in. The space is where the air is that the food is breathing, and you will know the space when you eat the food, you see, whatever comes from. You should eat food [grown] locally. [The local environment knows the needs of the local people. The seeds know. The seeds and water and the earth know what's needed for those around.] You've been told that for years now, at least one hundred, and you don't do it. So you are breathing foods, and foods are breathing you from other levels of consciousness that are not associated with your community at all! You have no (how you say?) thread of reference with the space you have been graced with.

You Are Eating Your Breath

The knowledge of space is a difficult understanding. You put structures up, and you say that is your space. Yet there is more to it. You're in it, you're around it, you're about it, and you're through it. You're in the interior of Earth. You're on all of the planetary systems that you can see, or you wouldn't be able to see them. You're on Jupiter, you're on Mars, you're on Venus, you're on the Sun, you're on the Moon, you're on Pluto, you're on Uranus, and you're on Neptune. You're on all of them — all of them, now, same time!

The breath you are breathing is a localized breath in consciousness — localized meaning countries. The point is that you are breathing consciousness. That is the point. Now, if you knew what the consciousness truly was in those arenas, you might choose not to breathe that because it is an expression of atomistic philosophy — electrons, stick protons, and that sort of thing. But you are an inconsistent being in the human condition. We are going to call it that way. You are not consistently yourself!

You go through your chakras of forty-nine personalities, and that's just something to let you be aware that you have personalities in each chakra, and they have to work with the other personalities in the other chakras. That's the basics. But the secret of your life is in the breath. You can go without water for a few days, but breath you can't. If you really understood this process called thought, you would concern yourself with who is breathing you and, "How do I breathe through this energy? What am I using to breathe?" Well, you know, it's a muscular function in your own personality: Breathe in, and breathe out. But where is this inadvertent breathing? You have burps and, what you say, pass your gas and things. There's a breath there coming out of you. How? From where? Why? You don't even correlate it. Well, in your acid reflux and the burps and some of the things you eat, you can correlate it to what you eat, but it's not a consistent idea to you. You only reflect on it when there is a discomfort within the system, and then you might check.

But if you are going to find out truly what you are doing here, you are eating your breath. The foods breathe through you. They breathe the space that they knew, that they grew up in. They have memory. They have memory. So this is the push, I'll say, to the organic systems. You are aware that your pesticides kill you and the insecticides and all of that. But now you're going to move into a different idea of growing: Food provides the interior breath for you, the breathing portions of your being that you can't see. All of your systems require oxygen inside. The lymphatic system, the pituitary, the liver, and the kidneys all require oxygen. There is a breathing component there. They all breathe in you.

The human condition is not aware that the heart breathes; the lungs breathe. Well, they are aware of their lungs breathing. They think the lungs just suck in air and then push it out. Then you have the liver that breathes, kidneys that breathe, and pancreas that breathes. All of your organs, they breathe. Your foods provide those breaths for those organs.

Right now, the human condition basically understands itself as a garbage disposal. You take everything in, and push it out. Take everything in; push it out. You're not aware of the function of it within the system. Grapes provide what you would say is an understanding of a beautiful breath. Hence, the wine concept. It can alter your consciousness, grapes. The same with any of your fruits and vegetables. They will alter your consciousness if you pay attention to the fruits or the vegetables that you are eating, and it is providing you breath. Not just sweetness and the taste of the fruit and the texture of it, but it is providing breath for the interior portion of your being. And what you are going to understand later, much later, is that you are the breath in the space that you are so that everyone else can breathe. That is the nature of the silver dragon. That's the nature of it. It becomes sparkling water.

Your auras become like the sparkling of water or the sparkling on top of your oceans or lakes. That interaction there, that interface, is where you are heading. Consider yourself the water. The sparkle is just in front of you, and there is an interface there coming. We are calling that the silver dragon for you right now. It is related to the polar energy — P-O-L-A-R, poles — the North Poles and South Poles of your planets: planets, plural.

Your Silver Divine Energy

As the body consciousness and the personalities within the body understand their uniqueness — for each is unique in the chakras, each is unique — and in that capacity of its uniqueness, it has authority in those realms. These seals are the seals that are put on the chakras when the authority has been given. You will see them. They are impressed (how you say?), not implanted. It's like …

Engraved?

You have wax, and you push a seal in it.

A stamp?

It is like that, only it's there already. It's just that the wax is going to melt, and the seals show. That's the way it is. Then they all have the authority in the realms. The heart chakra has the authority in this realm. The throat chakra has the authority in this arena, and this, that, and the other, because you are communicating with the same likeness in each one. There is no confusion. Everyone sees the same seals and knows what it is because he or she is being breathed by it, being breathed by it. You are being breathed by it.

You're going to understand that the chakras are reclaiming themselves, we're going to say it that way, and then the totality of the form is reclaimed by the entity allowing the chakras to reclaim themselves, because they know what they are supposed to do and how they are supposed to behave. It is the ego that runs away. We'll call it the ego, but it's not what you would say is the ego. It's another influence that wants you off your path. It wants to influence you as one who can be influenced. It's just up to determination. You don't realize this, most beings, until you are on your deathbed to hear the clack in the throat.

Your choices are limited then, but now in the human condition, you have the freewill ability to activate all choices. But it must be done inside, not out here. The human condition is not aware yet which antenna they are receiving, what data from within their consciousnesses, called the human physical. You have several antennae that you tune into. The ones that are reliable are the ones that understand it in here, base camp.

Heart.

Heart. The heart chakra and solar plexus, between the two. Your Buddha one who sits there in the pyramid of your soul is trying to get everything to the center. The heart in your evolutionary process is moving ever so slowly to the center of your being, from the left moving over to the center.

It is going to come from behind the sternum, and that is where the power of the drumbeat takes place. You all have a beat, and you will beat according to that process. It creates, as you heard, beats. It creates rhythms, and when you understand the rhythm and the beat, you understand there is an intent before that. When you intend the beat, the heart creates it, and people walk in that space. That's how it's done. You walk in the space of the masters. The masters are beating that beat. You feel it, and then you are trained to do that.

Evolutionary-wise, the heart is physically going to move to the center. It is now 2° to 3° off to the left. This is the evolutionary process of, we're going to call this, the silver dragon. The reason we're saying that is because it has motion and has concepts and has determination. It knows its job. Yet this is what beings would call the silver cord in old times because they could not see the expansion of the dragon from the twist, and its coming out and it's relating to the energy in your spines. When you are in that force, you could be in any space and time. Literally, the body will disappear and go into another place, and you are going to learn how to do that. At this time, it is not appropriate because right now you're working with space and you're understanding the grace of the space.

Now, when you activate the dragon, the silver one, a lot of sparkles start appearing all over. Those are beings in the other realms who are aware of the dragon energy and are aware of the purpose of it. They are looking for the graduation phase because when it enters the physical, everything shines. Everything will start ringing, actually. It has a very high pitch. Glass will crash or break. It can break. You have heard singers sing a pitch and the glass breaks. That kind of pitch will come into the body. Your body will sing it. You are in the regulating process of that. That is what all this training is about because it is called responsibility — responsibility — for where you are at.

Your position in space and time with your silver divine energy, you are responsible for that position in space and time, whatever is going on around there, because you are then coming in control of the space and the grace. That is the symbolism of a circle with the cube in it. Everybody's going cubic now, and you need to hold it, the cubic function, in a way, like the black cube of Mecca. It's the pelvis. You keep your pelvis cubic, and the functions start coming in correctly. You cannot bring it up. It has to stay down there, and then the pyramid form of the stupa, as you call it, is built on it. Then you change the color as you come up.

That's what you're doing. The reason you have stupas with Buddhas in them is to show you how to do it. That's what Buddha does. It shows you how to meditate. Building stupas will show you how to do it with the physical form. You are the stupa, and as you move into your buddhic form, you're going to the sixth seal. You will feel and see the Buddha, and then you will come and sit down in yourself in your Buddha form and carry your stupa with you. So there's a period where it's going to get heavy, and you have to move differently.

You're going to have to keep your spine erect because you have proprietary information now, and proper behaviors are required. You're not even going to be able to think like the others as this change takes place because your thinking will be more bodhisattva, to be of assistance to people in their suffering in the manner that they should know it. You're already supposed to know this. What are you doing? Are you having fun doing that? Stop. So the process of death is a learning process of what life really is, wherever it is.

You are feeling that understanding now, and everyone's going through it. This is the energy. It is what is going on in your movement here. You have a place, and you have time now, these weeks of this time.

August 2015

August. In this time of your third week in August, which is going to get interesting energy-wise, your breath is going to change. Your ability to breathe is going to change. By that, I mean you realize you are going to have to breathe differently. You're going to have to slow yourself down and breathe in a contemplative form.

You'll take a breath, and you're going to have to contemplate what was in that breath, not what you thought, not what you were thinking. "What was in the breath I just breathed?" Something was there. Some form of consciousness is there in the breath. So when you breathe, you will start saying peace to all beings. Peace to your being. Peace. You're breathing peace. Then you become aware of the selective nature of your processing as you breathe peace.

You become aware of it, and then what you will find out is the entity of peace starts coming around more and more to be breathed by you as peace. Then the concept is merged, and you know what peace is and the power of it. That's how it works. That's how it works, and you are feeling it now. The peace enters. It has entered, and it's working there. Sometimes some beings think peace can get boring, but peace is not boring. Peace has a beauty of health and nurturing all systems within the construct of the body. That's what peace does in the breath, and that's why trees are so important, because they sit still and continually breathe. They use the water, and they are a pump for you. You have the ability to move, but you are trees. This is a Kabbalah system. You have been told you are trees of light. There are teachers who teach that. How many times do you have to hear it? You are a tree, movable, and the tone of your "treeness" is in your bones.

You have a tone there that was given to you with intent. That means it has the ability to function and will manifest that intent. That intent is in your bones. It's related to the first letter of your name. We have gone through that over and over. The importance of that first letter has really not been emphasized enough in any culture because that is the start of the tone of yourself as you know yourself in this lifetime, pretty much.

What happens with beings, at times, when they change their names, is they are trying to get a different tone, or they will work with a different tone. But it is not what the bones knew or know of. So the bones have to adjust or try to adjust. They can't do it, actually. They have to put up with it because there is not a resonance there they were created with.

Sorry to bring that piece of information up. But you are going to have to understand that because the bones are what allow you to walk so that you are not a puddle or not sitting like a tree, not movable. The bones are one of the clues here, and that is what manufactures the blood for you. They have a consciousness, and what happens within the bones, you command the bones. Actually, you prophesy to the bones. That is what you were told to do. You talk to your bones. You command them to heal, to be (what you say) comfortable and strong. Then you need to understand what provides the sustenance and breath for the bones. In your world, the breath for the bones is calcium; that's what the bones breathe. That kind of interaction now, beings take calcium for the bones, and they don't even know. But if you knew the bones breathed it, you would be in a whole different space. The healing process would take place much faster.

The Continuity of Consciousness

Beings have difficulty communicating with other beings on your physical planet. When you first start communicating with the beings within yourself, you can get the system working correctly, because all interior beings communicate with all interior beings and everybody else, and they're all confused. They all know it, and that is why nobody says anything.

Now we start with peace. You're in a meditation. You're always in a meditation, whether you're waking or sleeping. You just don't know that yet. Your bones know it, and they are here to produce continuity in your self. It is called the continuity of consciousness from one lifetime to another lifetime to the present lifetime to the moment of next. Then the moment of next is always the moment of now. But you don't know that yet. You are just simply looking from one of your four directions. That's all, basically, from your higher self's perspective and from one of your four faces. But the integration is occurring now, literally, in 2015, and it's going to continue. It's not going to stop in 2016, 2017, and so on.

One of the reasons you're becoming concerned about your atmosphere is you're beginning to realize the importance of breath. You think it's the human consciousness breathing body-breath. It is in part, and you're destroying it, in part. There is also another part of you that is waking you up inside that you are breathing all things, literally. You just forgot it. Some provide benefits, and some don't. Even breathing thoughts, some provide the opportunity for wisdom and knowledge; most don't.

But you don't know how to separate through the sieve yet: Which antenna is working? Why that antenna? Why doesn't it go all the way down to the heart chakra? Why is it just spinning up here?

Around the head.

Around the head. Or why is it not going down to the pelvis and down your spine? Why doesn't your spine want to feel it? It wants to run away from some of these things. All of this is in front of the human condition right now.

The Pamphlet for Life is your self. You have your own little scorecard, and you're keeping track. Breath is the key. The foods that you eat breathe for you interiorly and help you. Be careful what you are eating, and know the breath in it. That is why you should pray or say a prayer over your food before you eat it because it might've come from a place that needed conditioning or prayers, all of that. You're supposed to know what you're doing in consciousness, being a spiritual being. Yet you're influenced by thought, and it's not your thought at all, either. It's someone else's.

The human condition's unique ability with thought is pristine and knowledgeable only unto itself, unless it wants to share with others. Then there is health to the body, mind, and spirit, and you move comfortably in the space that you are in with grace, because the space is the grace from your higher self's perspective. Otherwise, you are just floating around with all those other photons wondering what you're going to hit. If you can go through it, watch out for those neutrinos. They show up all over the place.

So you are moving through the human condition with knowledge of the human condition, different races, different colors, you call them, races, different. You're still the human condition, and the understanding of the differences of the colors has to come about yet. You are still doing this "mine is better than yours" thing. It's all the same. It's all the same — all the same.

The color is appropriate for the environment you are in, specifically as a protection from the poisons and thought processes that are available, that are not yours. The color has a defensive tone there. You are not aware of that. You take it personally and judgmentally, but you are born in a place, and it's the consciousness of the place. You must understand this: Each country has a different level of consciousness. Well, I shouldn't say "level." I should say different consciousness. The minute I say "level," people start comparing things. It's a different form of consciousness, yet it is consciousness in the human condition. You are realizing that in culture now. You should've realized that many thousands of years ago instead of the combative, confrontative force. That's the other being forcing that on you, bleeding through, how you say that?

Bleeding through?

Bleeding through, coming through, entering through, possession.

Okay, I understand.

That sort of thing is going on now, and the possessors and the ones being possessed are becoming aware of it.

"Where are all these negative thoughts coming from?" they say sometimes. I say, which antenna are you listening to? Don't be listening to some of those antennae. Turn that one off. You have things to do, and it's termed (as they have said) health to the body, mind, and spirit. That's the process of your self now.

The churches are doing their thing, in a manner, to create some level of education. But you're going to have to *apply* that teaching. The application of those teachings within any system is very difficult. They work within the system when the ones know the teachings to apply within that system. But to take the application to another system when they don't understand those teachings can be confusing. That's why right now you're getting all this other thing going on. A global war, a global catastrophe, you're trying to get started here. It won't be pleasant. The only thing available that you will have is breath. When you're sleeping at night, you can breathe, "Thank you, God. I can still breathe!"

You Can Handle It

The confusion is coming; it's really confusion. You're going to see so many extraterrestrials and UFOs flying around that you're not going to know what to do. But it's not them. They're trying to shift your consciousness so that you stabilize your planetary systems here through peace, protection, and joy in prayer. You're on the planet to help it, not to destroy it. But it seems to be going the other way around. You are going to face it. The human condition is going to face what they have done, and it's a sad thing here. You are going to have to learn to stop it! Some people do not believe until it's too late.

This is the time of Noah, the same thing. They didn't believe. You're in that thing now. You're right there. Same loop that Noah was in. Only this time, the animals know more than you do, and they're communicating. If you listen, your birds are speaking words, and they are not parrots. They are communicating an energy that you must pay attention to, and right now they're speaking, "Calm it down. Don't get so excited. Don't worry about it at all. Don't worry what they are protesting about." They are trying to reassure you fledgling, fowl — F-O-W-L — that you will make it. You don't have your wings yet.

So they're pushing that through there verbally in English for those who will listen. You will hear it. And when you hear it, don't let it upset you or shock you. That has always been the case. You're just tuning it differently. That is what is occurring now. Beings are hearing them. Nature is warning the human condition to calm down and don't get all excited. "You can handle it," basically. That is what is occurring now.

That is another importance of trees; the birds can nest in them safely. That is what you are doing with your own physical consciousness, but you don't know it now. You are creating and building this tree. You are this tree that eventually the little birds will be able to flock to and nest in, literally, and the little birds in your world are the children. Children instinctively love trees.

The Next Level of Breath

We have one more level to work through for breath. The next area is going to be your sternum. It is going to start to breathe, and you might feel a tingling there or an itching. It might itch in the sternum, and that is going to create a tone, or a beep, possibly, a breath. It's looking for, as you make your telephone calls, a response. "Someone, pick up the phone!" When the sternum functions this way, it will send the tone back to the spine, right in the back of the spine, right to the center of the heart chakra. That will bring an energy vortex from the bottom of the sternum up to your heart and to the top of what is your throat chakra, here, the clavicle. It will create an angle, like a bow, and you will feel it pulling the heart energy to the center — not the heart itself, but the energy there. It will feel like a bowstring being pulled, and when it does, you breathe that down. You breathe that down because the heart knows it's going to move, and it's cautious about it. You need to be cautious with it. So this is one of the techniques you're going to use.

The bowstring: Pull it in gently. It will hit the coccyx. It'll go right up to the crown chakra, and then you're sitting with your self. You might as well begin to learn some mudras because you are going to use them when you are in your public, whether you know it or not. Just sort of gently move your fingers correctly because that's the exhale of the breath that is being breathed from the inside of you.

Mudra, it is like a warning to others, that they know there is a difference here, because, really, you're moving from visible to invisible. But you have to be cautious with this. Many have died and not understood the process when they are working through this shamanic tradition. We are not going through that process. You've already heard "you are as dead now as you will ever be," but we don't need to prove that. You are becoming more alive now, and you have the willingness to understand that you are a test tube, basically, in the human condition learning moreness. You are coming out of the test tube. The opening of yourself is taking place, the treasure chest, the glory part of your being that you know that you are. That is present everywhere, like this force here is moving, is moving.

You Have Come a Long Way

We are in a difficult process right now because everyone wants to learn, but they don't know what to learn. "Remember the breathing ones" is a good phrase to contemplate. Remember the breathing ones because when you're dead, you don't breathe. You're out of the body in another level of consciousness. You're floating around in a lightbody, bouncing around all over the place, looking for some place to be stable. But you don't breathe. You're thinking most of the time and having reactions to what you see because you're seeing and reacting and being placed.

The nature of breath is significant in the understanding of the Holy Spirit because your bones breathe the Holy Spirit and produce the blood for you. So you are in a literal understanding of your own manufacturing process. You're living it. Pretty soon you're going to learn not to be influenced by others words or thoughts because you have your own that are pristine and powerful and used to build civilizations, really, or have been in the past, just by doing something. Then someone else will come along and see you doing something, and they'll want to participate or perhaps throw you off the track. But eventually you keep doing, keep doing, because you're the only one doing it. Keep doing it. It is your breath. It is your (what you call) path to magnificence; that is what you are to begin with. You're learning that now as you breathe continually.

In this day and age, most of you can't believe you made it this far, as it is. How did you get this far? It comes from the genius of the phrase you call God, the being you call God. He knows. She knows. They know. It is known, and it is purposeful. It is intended, and it is (what you term) a rescue mission to assist those who want to be assisted. We are not forcing ones but rather assisting those who want to be assisted. They'll know because they'll come for the assistance. They'll feel it. They'll be guided to it. That's what's occurring now on your planet all over. That's why the Dalai Lama is doing a lot of traveling now.

CHAPTER

6

Breathe Thankfully – You Made it to October

August 11, 2015

You have a lot of confusion. It's all over the place. Now, what's happening is the divineness is separating ones who have the ability to understand and perform within themselves their own special flavor, which is in your name. And your bones resonate to it and *know* the power of it. That is why I have said before, the first letter of your name is very important. It sets the tone for your self.

If you understood the significance of the intent of the tone in your bones, then you would understand your life's progress. Actually, you would have an advantage because you would know what your history is to be, but you beings, say, see your future. You would already know what it is. It's really not your future. You're in it, and you're doing it. So that's why health to body, mind, and spirit is important.

You beings in the physical world are not really aware that you are being influenced by the invisibles. You're caught up in your words, *not in the feelings of your bones*. You have intelligence in your (and this is where your intelligence is) little finger; it's the mind's force. You have intelligence in your muscles and your sinew, which move the bones. You have intelligence as you say this.

So you clear yourself and push two fingers, push two fingers. You're going to learn the importance of your fingers — not just to grab and pull, "It's mine." No. It is to understand. You have heard of Qigong. Each finger has an important process in your electrical current.

As you move your piano — what I call your piano — your fingers are the keys, and if you move them one after the other daily for a few minutes, you will find you are playing a different note. And someone from inside you is realizing that you are recognizing the importance of the movement of the fingers for self.

The Human Condition Has Been Set Aside by the Divine

You are going to have to understand the acceptance of each being for the other. The arguments are occurring within your self, and they are caused by other beings who are aware of you and also very jealous of the human condition because they are not human. The human condition has been set aside by the Divine for special reasons. You have been told this and told this and told this. There is a being who does not like that unification, because when it happens, the power within you becomes greater than that particular being who is causing the discomfort — the pain and the agony and the killings.

You have (what you term) your temple. You have seen your stupas. You are the stupa. Your Buddha one sits in you. When you see a stupa, there is a Buddha, and the stupa is the representation of the soul; the soul is in the pyramid. You sit there as the Buddha form, as a Buddha one — legs crossed, and everything golden energy. You felt that in the back. That's how you begin to understand another level of communication that is beyond telepathy. It's the emotion empathy: You will feel the emotion of that expression and understand it.

You know what it is you don't need — the refractions and the hard contact for confirmation — because you're moving more into your etheric form and into your physical form. There's an interface now. You are at the interface. You're getting ready — well, some of you are getting ready — to disappear your self and reappear. You're going to have to know how to do that. It's a simple matter of center and peace to all beings when you center. Peace to all beings. It creates a peace in the soul aspect. You have seen it in your bodhisattvas.

You are setting yourself up or receiving bodhisattva energy. It will come into you, and it will, she will (blue bodhisattva), come in and adjust herself in you so that the posture is correct. She knows what the exact position is. You might feel your hand being contorted in a different way, but she is doing it, and it won't be you, as you won't know how to do it.

You are learning how to communicate with the bodhisattvas, the angels (you've heard the names of some), and other beings in the spiritual realm that want to assist you in the accumulation of your own power — your own accumulation of your power. For this is the unification when you do that — allow yourself to do that now. You'll feel it. Just push your fists together, and then when you do open, you should feel energy go up the back of your head for acknowledgment. This is tricky because it can be disconcerting, but as it comes up to the back of the head, you're going to be before your birth in the identity of you before you were incarnated, before you even came into the womb.

As the fetus was growing, you were not always there. You are ready to join your self from other levels, regardless of what others think. The time for fitting in social consciousness is over. The development of the individual self and knowledge of your own individual power within self is what's coming up, the reliance on it. To know you have accumulated a sense of safety — and that's what this is — is a thankfulness for the safety within the form that you are in. You know it, and the other beings around you know it.

The Human Condition Is Precious

We are having a difficult time now communicating from the invisible world to the physical, visible world, for the eyes react to sight. The sight creates an expression within the self. You do know that you react when you see things. It's always that way. So that is the importance of flowers. They're innocent. They grow with water. They grow. You're a flower. You are flowers. You are more than that. You are tones and songs and colors, and that knowledge is coming about so that everyone can walk as a flower in his or her own essence without, what you term, worrying about the criticism of others.

Become aware of what you're really saying, to whom you are saying it, and why you are saying it. You are backing up beyond preacher mode. Now, you're not preachers. You're going to be learning to distinctly work with the energies so that others understand why you are here. And what you are really here for is the service to others, not yourself, because once you serve others and assist them, you actually help yourself.

Because the human condition is a precious condition, it does not exist anywhere else, not even on, what you term, the ships. You need another body to get into the human condition, and then you try to transition into what you call a precious world, precious world. And it's so precious that you are going through a cleansing process now. The world is being cleaned — literally. The Divine Feminine now is ordering her house to be put in order. That's the magnetic flux you are feeling in the planet; that's the goddess energy. The goddesses know when things are out of order. Whether they correct it or not is another story.

The incarnated goddess knows that she should have things in order for a reason, because it is a sign of her perpetuosity. The ability to continue forever and ever, she knows that. And that's why all these volcanoes are going off. She is cleaning house. That's why the weather's changing. Weather is an effect of consciousness. Sunspots are a reflection of your thoughts globally coming back at you. The Moon slows down the emotional forces, what you're feeling emotionally. That is what everyone has been feeling this month [August 2015]. Haven't you been feeling a little strange daily? You're wondering sometimes whether you're even going to make it to the next day energy-wise. What was that about? What's happening? The space is shifting.

There is a being called Space who gives you the opportunity to be in grace to learn yourself. Space is the grace. Space is the grace, and it is cubic. You can see it. You move within it. You are like a sphere that is within the cube. And you are going through the expansion process with this. Everyone is; and everyone is looking for the safety net of consciousness and love, the safe feeling that love is there, and it is safe there in love — not the Sodom and Gomorrah type of love or this other stuff that's going on here.

Your World Consciousness Varies

There is a sense of safety of a bird in its nest in love — a baby bird in a nest — and that's what you are. You're little birds now and about ready to fly. If you could, understand this concept here of the nest: You're the bird of the nest and love being in the nest because you know nothing else. The paramount reason for your expansion is the knowledge of the nest, and then you come out of it. It comes from the solar plexus. This wants out, yet it is sent back to learn more. So you are doing in and out, in and out, but you are going to be in it and stay in. Understand, it's a simple joy of looking at another human and animals. But there is a joy there.

The inside of you has a fear of looking out because of the old conditioning. It goes back down, and it comes up and peeks and looks because it has not been allowed to really show itself without fear in judgment of everything and everyone. But you are going through that. You have come out of the ground flower-wise, the bud stage, and you're about ready to bloom — you all are — in a way that's different and accepted by everyone who's in the same garden, we'll say. You're there.

A lot of the great difficulties we have in explaining these things is segregation of consciousness in religious concepts — different religion "here," different religion "there." You also have that in countries. France is different in consciousness from Germany. Germany is different in consciousness from Yugoslavia. Consciousness in Yugoslavia's different from consciousness in Brazil. The United States has a different level of consciousness, which is basically, what is termed, the "expression of free will here" more than in other countries because of their restrictions. But for the United States, I have to say, this has caused the country some problems in certain areas, interfering in other units of consciousness.

Eventually you're going to find it's all the same consciousness. It's a jurisdictional phase. Religion is like crowd control. Hold it "here," hold it "here," and hold it "here." Same truth but different authority over the use of control, not for blessings and freedom and health. But you're going to overcome that. The secret of your birth is in the religion of your parents. You came in to correct and take the wisdom from the peace, whatever religion, it doesn't matter.

You knew before you were born what it was, and you aligned your self with the spiritual forces of the planet in your astrological chart. Now, you have heard about the holographic universe. Your astrological chart is imprinted on your back, so you say, and it has been said that it is a holographic image coming from invisible space pushing through you. It is there, so your higher self sees it, and all the spiritual forces working with you can see it, and they know the opportunities and things available for you. They are watching the individual ego self make its choices through these things. Now you are going to go right back into that.

You're in this expansion being watched by your self. If you could allow your selves to see your self, through your self, then you would see all your paradigms — all your choices, all your setups and destiny — yet you shouldn't. Destiny is a precious thing to you, and to you only, because it is a thing you said to the Divine before you came here that you would try to accomplish. It's called the mission. And you just keep going till you get the pieces correct because when you leave, you have to show yourself what you've done with the free power given to you.

You think you know how to breathe, but you don't know how to do it when you're sleeping. It's an unconscious thing. You say "subconscious" thing. But there are many beings in you in the spiritual realm. There are 144,000; it's more than that — 144,000 friends, or divine forces, within you to assist you. That's the ascension concept. They know what they're doing. You just have to allow yourself to understand.

There is a relationship between that and twelve and also for the twelve months of the year and so on. When you do these things, you're accepting yourself in the present. This is just peace to all beings. And when you have this moment, you can allow a flame to come up out of the right hand for you and then a flame out of the left hand. Then you've seen the angels with flames out of their heads, little fire, a little flame. You're like a candle in the darkness for others, with your kindness and your gentleness. They can sense it. You know what to do if it's hot. You just back up.

Discomfort and Illness

The discomfort and illness in the body is an argument with the Divine in your self. That's what you're doing. The recognition of your self and knowledge is to find out why, if you want to, and how to change it, how you change it. Are you willing to change it? Or are you going to sit and argue with yourself? Because that is what you are really doing when you have conflict with another being. You are just arguing with another part of yourself. You have not recognized that yet, that's all. So peace to all beings, and you have an opportunity, we'll say, to visit with the angels. Well, they actually visit with you.

You will find that you have a mission. You have a duty, and you are, in one manner, obligated because you're going to keep reincarnating until it's done or put in a place so that you can understand that you have an ability to think for yourself and be yourself, regardless of what anyone else thinks.

You are in that movement now, not just the physical flesh. I am saying that the bones are beginning to understand here — the bones — because if you didn't have them, you would have nothing. You wouldn't have muscle or sinew to attach to the bones. So you have to be thankful for all of your layers. The reason the flesh is covered by skin is because the flesh is really delicate and sensitive. It is a private self, so to speak, and is a breathing apparatus for the flesh. If you really know your flesh — your skin — you would have more pleasure for your self. This is what's causing some of the sickness in your society. They do not understand the wisdom of the body.

You Wake Up Daily with a Brand-New Body

It's not just your body. You have forty-nine personalities in that body, and each one belongs there. Then you have seven seals *and* the chakras. Each one belongs there. It is for the dignity of your self that this process, what you call in your world today in your August [2015], is taking place. This September and your next two weeks in August are going to become very interesting. By the time your October is here, you're going to breathe thankfully that you made it through there. You won't even remember some of this activity. You're already forgetting some of the things that happened a week ago. But you felt that energy force there, an invisible force that felt heavy. You're going to get through it. Take a breath. You're here. What happened? You don't remember.

In a manner, they are erasing your memories of concepts that aren't appropriate for right now. So you're starting a journey cleanly with basically a new body, a new body — a brand-new body — every twenty-four hours. As you wake up, you are going through a new body. You are getting a new body. The old body left. It took its dreams with it when you slept. That's what is really happening. You're coming into a new body. If you really knew that, you would understand the true beauty of yourself each morning. You get better looking every day. You do whether you think so or not. I don't mean looking in the mirror. I am talking about the interior portions of you that understand their own beauty and feel it, like it — a personal identification of beauty for the self, whether anyone else agrees or not.

Now, one of the hardest things to confirm within yourself is the presence of your own soul within you. That's the hardest thing. This finger, the mind finger, the little finger, will help you confirm that because you don't even know where your mind is. It's not here in your brain or in the head; it's behind you. That's why people think in the past all the time; you have had the experience that is an accumulation of mind stuff. You don't have a future experience yet. You have no mind for it. So the understanding of the mind, you had to go above it to see yourself in the process.

This is the primary one, this one right now, for your basic understanding. You're in your pyramid; it creates a pyramid force. Pyramids are there because you can't roll a pyramid. You can roll cubes, rectangles. You try rolling a pyramid, and it's not going anywhere. So you are there now; you are there now. You are a representation of consciousness of your genetic line. You're the ones who have to fix it because it hasn't been done yet. When you accelerate, you pull all your genetic codes together in there with you. You're the one who's available now for spiritual understanding of the past — and your family, everyone in your genetic line. They are your tribe. What it's for is you're all becoming tribal. You all belong in a position within the tribe. That knowledge now is going to be useful. It is what saves lives. It saves beings, and it saves souls.

God's Path Is in the Water

There is a difference between the life in a being and the soul. The integration is what you're going through now, that pleasure of the breath. You can go without water for a few days, but you can't go without breath. Life is in the breath. If you understand the words that "God's path is in the water," you will understand the significance of the water. Breath and water provide your body, breath allows your speech, and water allows your electrical current; it moves right through the water. There's knowledge there. Your bones know it, your muscles know it, your flesh knows it, and your sinew knows it. All your lymphatic systems — you have more than one — know it. Each organ came from the same seed; consciousness separated them for different functions, and you are it. Now you are going through the knowledge of how you did it.

It was a requirement that you had a mother for a body. You are going to learn the significance of what mother really means. There is a nurturing aspect there; whether you enjoyed your mother or not, it doesn't matter. There is a nurturing aspect that gave you bones. That acknowledgment is of historical significance for you to understand — if you just understood it. I don't mean just genealogy-wise. I'm talking about the relationship you were born in. You chose that for your own specific reasons, for the hidden wisdom there that you forgot about last time in that particular scenario. Your bones know it, and as they start pushing out the information, you will know it too. That is the process that the human condition is in now. You're going to find out you're only arguing with yourself from listening to all the other stuff going on.

You are precious entities beyond imagination. That acknowledgment now is important to understand for the health of the body, mind, and spirit. Peace to all beings. All right, we are through.

CHAPTER

7

Humanity Is Being Given the Opportunity to Pass through the Gate

August 18, 2015

One of the most difficult things for the human condition, body physical, to understand is the penetration and walking through two different things — the invisible forces that are beginning to make their presence known more. Now, walking through is what you do daily. You're just walking in space and don't understand that there are beings in between, other physical constructs. You have the idea of "this is it; this is the environment." Yet the invisibles now are — I am going to say it this way, and perhaps there might be an understanding — the invisibles (the guides, and so on, relatives who have passed, and all of this) are remembering their contracts with the physical. In particular, within particular human beings, there are contracts there. I will put it this way: Your contract is established in your horoscope. People look at a horoscope so that they can say they might know their future.

What you do not understand is the spiritual force is connected to the planets, literally your physical planet, and what in your astrological terms is the house that the spiritual force is in. It's not the planet that's there. The planet is just a physical representation of the spiritual force that is there to assist you with the particular definition of that house. Now, when you first come, we will say, to the first knowledge of the time of incarnation, you think you have the powers that you have, we will call it, out there in the spirit world. Here, same. Yet the limitations occur within the placement of the planets in the [astrological] house. That's where there are limitations. You thought you could do everything, but you forgot about the contracts.

So the resistance in the form is the argument with self yet the "forgettingness" of it. Yet the forgetting is truly forgiving. Otherwise, you would be beating yourselves up for past mistakes all over again. That's not the point. The point is to understand the energy. "I recognize this is what déjà vu is. I recognize this has altered the outcome because I am going through it again." So don't worry about altering the outcome. Well, think about altering the outcome, but actually stay in the space of recognition, center, and let whatever is occurring around you pass by. This is where you need to back up and observe.

There Aren't Enough People Praying

The process in your month now, this August and your September, is going to increase dramatically. By "process," I mean the introduction to the divine spirit that really runs things. Your weather's changing dramatically, the volcanoes are going off; you already know that. The earthquakes are going off. California is going to be hit with a very big earthquake, but it's not the point of the earthquake. It's the point of when you knew it, and now this is confirmation that more movement is coming. That's just the beginning.

I have already told you of the meteorite that is going to strike in your Atlantic Ocean off the coast of North Africa. That's going to send a tsunami to the East Coast, literally. It is going to wipe out cities. The water is going to go to the Appalachian Mountains. But nobody believes it. Then how would you tell everyone to move? Well, you had better pay attention to the understanding of spirit versus physical incarnation. This is what's occurring, and a tsunami is also going to hit California. It won't be pleasant. It won't be pleasant.

The point that is going to be brought up is that there are not enough people praying. Number one, they don't know what to pray. They don't know how to pray. They don't even like the word "prayer." They have to manipulate it so that it feels comfortable with their processes. Within prayer, there is a secret, and the secret is humility. That's it. That's it. It's a complete surrender to the self of self that wants to have (what you call) a dramatic influence in this incarnation — the incarnation. The secret of the divine influence in the incarnation is in the prayer.

It's the prayer that you used to be born, number one, because you answered your parents' prayer — whatever mode they were in and their concept of understanding of prayer and the thought process and the sexual act. All of that was your response. You answered those prayers. It works for all parents, yet they don't know they are praying. They are thinking these things, the response comes out of that, and you're there. That's how it works. But you're not aware of that. There are influences that provide the answer called yes to everyone who petitions. It's always yes — always will be, always has been. Yet you are not aware of your influences under the yes because the connection with the intent of thought is not there.

Words, but you don't even understand where your thoughts are coming from, and was that really you thinking? "How did I think of that, and what's the process?" The intent of breath, which is what gives you the life force and your blood, is to understand eternity and foreverness. It's in the breath.

What makes you breathe? Well, you say you breathe because it is an automatic reaction. It has to be when you sleep. Yet there is a being coming. It's the Holy Spirit. I will tell you that. It's going to breathe through you. It is going to come into your back and breathe [exhales] through you. It does not do the mediumship thing. It does not incorporate in the body and take over the body. It moves through all bodies at the same time, and it can and will (when it wants to) do that as a demonstration.

You will still be present in your form, but there will be a force that comes over you that speaks through you, and you'll know it wasn't you. Everybody sitting in the same circle is going to do the same thing to everyone at the same time. Then the confusion, "Oh, there really is, what we term, someone else here, some other process and force that knows what it's doing because I don't understand how that happened." That will be the reaction. Then there will be the running around, which is what everyone is doing right now.

You're having difficulty in understanding evil. You don't like to understand it as that word. You prefer to choose more charming influences to describe these things. Yet it is evil. It has not a desire to see the continuity of the human condition. It wants it done, over, dead, completely. Forget it. That force is what interferes with the concept of your intent of thought and the processing of information through the body. It causes the doubt and all of this thing. When doubt comes up, the quickest way to do it is to allow yourself to forget whatever it was because forgetting is forgiving, in a manner, of the self. So you don't have to go through the true surrender, I guess you would say, of the humility of self and having to forgive for misappropriate deeds. It is also forgiveness around your walking into a thought process. There is also a realm you are going to hit where there is no thought. You can't think; there won't be a thought. It is inappropriate to think, as you'll get a response you might not want. So you're in that now.

Your September, this coming next four weeks, is going to be incredibly significant and dangerous for ones if they don't understand what is really happening. Earth is going to, I don't want to say "crack," but it will be a crack, and it's going to feel like it all over the planet at the same time, at the same time. When it does, the use of your politicians is going to be exposed, and your armies and warrior beings. You're going to be more into the influence of rescuing than killing. There's going to be so much damage that belief systems are going to be rocked. You're going to need to have water available.

Three Days of Darkness

You're going to get three days of darkness; I will put it that way. I might as well bring it right up. There will be no sun for three days. There will be necessity for candles. The necessity for candles is so that you can maintain a continuity of your own consciousness present in the dark. If you don't, the darkness will overcome you. These are the ones that don't want success for the human condition.

There are seven spirits in the divine force:

1. the spirit of the Lord shall rest upon Him [Yahweh]
2. the spirit of Wisdom
3. the spirit of Understanding
4. the spirit of Counsel
5. the spirit of Might
6. the spirit of Knowledge
7. the spirit of the Fear of the Lord

Yahweh, we'll say, and the last one is Fear. The last one is Fear, the spirit of Fear, and it is fear. That's the humiliating condition of repentance that will come over ones. It is going through the first spirit as love, because it loves everything. It is correcting its children. I am saying "it" because you beings have difficulty with personalities and constructs in male and female things. That's not the point now. The point is breath and life because you are going to find out, each one of you, this is what is going on in your secular world, men changing themselves into women and women are turning themselves into men. If you don't, you understand that you are all male and female, whether you get that process or not. It is still a polarity thing you are working on. It is not in relation to the sexual content at all; it's not the point at all. There is a union that occurs within the physical that allows you to be noticed by your self, the one that is inside. There is this desire to be noticed and recognized for the thing that is going on here.

The desire for recognition will switch your understanding of your sexual orientation. You have to remember what your sexual orientation is and that you are the process of extreme potency in your bones — in the bones, not the skin, not the flesh, not the tendons, and not the sinew. Those processes allow the bones to move. The bones are the foundation, so you're getting the construct of acknowledging, whether you like it or not, your bones. You are going to eventually acknowledge your bones as being the primary source of your connection to the Holy Spirit because that is where the blood comes from, and that is what the Holy Spirit rides upon to influence the conditions of breath in the system. The blood breathes. So you're in a clinical understanding of your self, and the pains are going to remind you that you are not in the proper form, not in the proper position, and not in the proper thought processes.

The Secret Lies in the Wisdom of Nature

The activation now that is going on is occurring here in the solar plexus. This is where your Buddha one sits. This is the one that is really in charge of the concept. Your body is a stupa. It's like the Buddhist's stupas, and in there is a Buddha one sitting there. All the mysteries of your self are inside here, your stupa. You are walking with a tremendous amount of force now, so you have to balance all of it in all directions. There are six: front, back, left, right, up, down. You are in the middle of that cube of your memories and of your future desires. You are in the middle of it. You are in that cube of space. That is your cube.

Now space herself is shifting, and I'm saying "her." Herself is shifting. She is shifting, so the cubes can see a greater light, even in, what you call, the ignorance of the self. So as she shifts, we're going to call the wandering ones, the humans, not the animals. The animals know what is going on; you can see the changes in them. The wandering ones, the humans who don't understand the natural condition, are going to have panic attacks, fear, craziness. The balance for this craziness is your trees. They are going to stay there unless there is a great wind or an earthquake that knocks them down or lightning splits them in half, whatever. But the trees will be your understanding.

Wood is your fifth element because it's a pump. Trees, they pump oxygen, which is what you breathe. So the significance of your self in the trees needs to be felt, not just mentalized. This needs to be felt. Your bones need to thank the trunk of the tree because the trunk of the tree can remind the bones how the process works in breath. The bones don't pump water, but in the breath, they understand.

Now, the secrets of self, any self, lies in the wisdom of nature, lies in the wisdom of nature. Wisdom and understanding are two different things. One is the application, and one is the knowledge of the application. You are going through this right now. When these systems crash — I am talking about your computer systems — you are going to have very much difficulty.

It's going to become important to understand the nature of the tribal Americans here, what you call your Indians here. They held and are still holding sacred energies, not all. In a manner, the Indian country (what you call spaces) in your United States, the territories of the Indians, are going to be the safe places for Americans. The Indians have already allowed that amnesty to those who got there. This is what is occurring in the spiritual realm. There are events that are going to happen that have been told about and talked about, but no one is paying attention. They don't know what to do, really, because you have been lulled into a false sense of security here.

The beings who are receiving this information (some are called prophets and things, not by themselves, however), they are given information, and they are told to spread that information, because if they don't, they will be punished first and then the others later. But then they won't have any repercussions coming to them. They just have the expressions of tears when no one believes and the results occur.

So the body physical, literally, is having this feeling of being shut down. Part of this spiritual force within the body does not want to be here because it knows what's coming. Yet the contract signed is that you will be because others do not even understand yet the necessity that is going to be required after these events. The sky's going to change color, earthquakes are going to happen, and fire is already running rampant.

The sky's changing color, the oceans are going to react, and your earthquakes, the planet-cracks thing, tilts. You won't even know.

When it hits like that, your whole consciousness will shift because the space shifts and everybody else's consciousness shifts just to stay in the right space. So you need to have your spine centered. You are already getting the fire concept, fires going on, explosions all over the world. You are killing yourselves, and you are eventually going to wake up to it. You're going to find out who is influencing you. Well, that's just the beginning. That's just the beginning.

After this, your September, when these devastations take place, you are going to have one come up, what you term the antichrist (that's your word), a new-world-leader thing. Be careful with that one. It is going to look like he helped everyone, but you are going to find yourself in a concentration camp mentally. In the ability to think, he will be controlling thought. You have to learn to understand the real thought is within yourself — the sacredness of yourself, the blessings of yourself, and the concept of peace to all beings. When you call those forces, the peace to all beings, you set up perimeters in your area and your space, and the divine, we'll call it, and the Holy Spirit will come through to ensure that for you.

You're going to need to move into another direction now, not just, "the Father, the Son, and the ..." You're going to need to understand the Holy Spirit, the invisible one that can be visible. This is beyond ... in your world, the laws are you can insult the father, you can insult the mother, you can insult Mohammed and Jesus, and all of them, Buddha, whatever you can get away with. You will be forgiven for it. But you can't with the Holy Spirit, because it is within you. It is what breathes you, what produces your blood, and what knows your worth. If it gets tired of your worth, it leaves, just leaves. That's all. It doesn't say anything. It just has a wish not to support that concept, basically.

The warnings are being given all over. You are having difficulty now, however, with your spiritual leaders because they are stuck in a paradigm of "this" church, "that" church, and "my church is better than your church." We did "this," "this," "this," "this," "this."

Karma Is the Result of Intent over Time

You have the same conditions in your United States today as was in Sodom and Gomorrah, and you know that story! The disbelief is that story was maybe not correct. The truth is it was, and you're in the same thing now! It's your privilege to have free will, you think. In the understanding of what is forever, you don't know how you came to have a body or were born to this time, really. You don't know where you came from out of the ethers, what systems. You have heard stories about it when people get caught up in this reincarnation thing and karma, but you don't really know what it is. You're seeing it from the other side of self right now with the karmic situation. The result: Karma is a result of intent and desires over what you beings call time. But time is collapsing.

Time is not a linear, horizontal thing. Time is a direction, and it is up, if you knew it yourself. You're going through that understanding of the importance of not damaging another because you create damage for yourself. This sequence (we're going to call it) that you are in is going to create a notification, particularly when you beings start seeing your northern lights. You've seen them there up north, but that type of phenomenon is going to start occurring all over the planet, colors in the skies — and I don't mean rainbows. You're going to see the wavy motion of these electrical forces. When you see them, believe it. That's a force. Also, believe there is another one pushing this force, or pulling it, and causing changes in consciousness.

Humankind has the ability to think in a moment and cure any disease it needs to. That's from the power of the God-self because there is no disease in the God-self. When humankind begins to understand that, they create a greater arena of space because as those come closer, they are healed. They are healed, and others are healed. And the space starts healing. There is a change in the abilities of pleasure in a way that sustains each and every one, not just a selfless concept of your self.

You are going to learn to think collectively and not for the result because the result will be at the beginning with the intent. You're going to learn to get beyond thought, understand what intent really is, and then bring it down. Then it spreads through the system. This is where your crystalline structure, which is your bones, begins to shine. Your auric field begins to expand, and your chakras open. You get all your seals, and you finally know something. You understand the importance of the breath. When the crown opens, as it's going to, it links with other crowns. But it also has an effect on the solar plexus and heart chakra at the same time.

There's a triplicity there that starts being cautious — not looking for, what you say, the teacher to come to you but that you are in connection with the teacher now. What's the problem? Why did you not remember that? Because everyone wants out of the classroom. It was like when you were in school, you were staring out the window at the playground, not paying attention to your teacher because there were windows there. This is the same thing.

You need to center now. The Great Teacher is coming. Everyone's looking for the second coming of the Christ and Maitreya and all of these others to save you. It doesn't work that way. They come to remind you. That's why Jesus gave the Lord's Prayer. He shortened it from the 150 psalms. Nobody knew how to do it. So he gave the Lord's Prayer, which is a condensation of the 150 psalms. It is a magical tool. You say, "Our Father," you pause, and there is an intent there, "hallowed be thy name." There is a whole other phrase in that thing, there, because it's just the pronunciation of a name, but everybody recognizes, and they look and they stop.

There are two alternatives: "thy kingdom come" or "let us go into thy kingdom." Pause. You have an understanding. Yet it is not taught that way, but Jesus did it. He condensed 150 psalms. I am telling you this because the magic is in the psalms. Those words were placed there by angels in the appropriate manner so that the result would happen. It's in the Koran too.

Certain religions are required for certain levels of consciousness. Let's put it that way. You're going through this distinction. Each one needs to find his or her own, and you need to find out that you are the religion. You are developing your own religion. That's what provided you your pathway to continue and still be alive. You're developing your own religion within you. You might not be the prophet-prophet, but you are becoming your own prophet. You know what you shouldn't have done, eventually, and how you can improve on your physical condition. It's the pain in the body that gets your attention more than words from other beings. So you know there needs to be a correction there.

There Is Opportunity for Miraculous Curings Now

Now, your pelvis — and a lot of beings are going through this — is literally a magic cauldron. You know the old witches in the caves brewing their stews in the cauldron? That's what you do in the pelvis. That's what it is there for. You bring up the forces of the fire, and you understand yourself. You begin to walk differently because you have to understand that the chakra at the bottom of your foot has to open and close appropriately when you walk. Beings don't even consider there is a chakra in the bottom of their feet, number one, and number two, they don't even consider their feet until they hurt.

You take advantage of all your systems until the system itself is in pain. Then you pay attention. The appropriate manner is to be thankful for the system when you wake up in the morning, all of them. Be thankful for the system when you go to bed, and be in a position, at least initially when you lie, to sleep flat so that the bones can recognize where they are and the stings.

The process of exorcism, which is becoming very popular now, is even hitting in the general population. Everyone is possessed a certain way, and some are trying to exorcise their demons by killing people. That's not going to work. They don't know what they're doing. That's a possession thing going on there on both sides. It's the ridicule of spiritual forces by the evil one, and they are caught up in it. They have no idea. They think they are thinking something very profound, and they're not. They haven't studied anything and barely thank the water they drink. They don't even do that, actually. So you're in another process here, literally.

The old world of social consciousness is going to go away. It is going to go away. The problem is … the way that is going to be achieved is the difficult part. There is going to be devastation. The when of it, it's close; that's all we can tell you. You'll want to be practicing to be in the space of safety.

You are going to begin to have these beings appear out of the sky and stand right in front of you. I'm talking about beings like Metatron and Sandalphon and Gabriel, these angels. They are not here to have a simple conversation. They are here to instruct. If you want to understand them, the force behind Gabriel, read the

Koran, and then you'll be thankful that you just have the Bible because there is a whole other jurisdiction going on there. Gabriel is the Angel of Truth, associated with the Moon. He is also justice. He knows it exactly. The Moon is associated with emotional behavior, the water — controls the water, the water in you, controls the oceans.

Gabriel is showing up. He is in the West. I have mentioned these positions before. Raphael's in the East. Uriel's in the North. Michael is in the South. To prevent total disorientation, find where the North Star is. That thing will never change. That will always be in the north, regardless of the shifting here. That is the gate out of limited consciousness. It is called the gate of Tarsus. That is Archangel Uriel's jurisdiction.

Humanity is being given, going through, the opportunity to pass through that gate. Not everyone will make it. There is going to be a sensation of craziness because you haven't learned to work with both sides of your brain at the same time. You haven't unified. There are seven conditions in your self. You are going through the arguments within self. That is why the bodies are going through pains. The one causing the pain — you say, "All right, I got the idea" — you know what it is? What's the correction? It'll be an electrical current, actually, a little switch that turns the thing off. You are supposed to have an idea of the proper foods to eat for the continuity of your system to be available for others, because you're here to save ones, not to ridicule and control. But that is what the majority in your world does or tries to do — control others. You can't. You can't, not with this force coming now.

You are in — I'm going to repeat it — very difficult times (I will call it), dangerous, depending on where you live. If you don't pay attention, you will know you didn't pay attention. And you will go through, "I should have." That is what will happen, and you will get another body somewhere else, as this cleaning process goes. The conditions you beings call hell are conversions of a perverted mind. Conversions going down there and trying to ... no. Center yourself.

Don't pay attention to what's around. Pay attention to what's up. You have an opportunity now for miraculous curings, I guess you would say, healings of your self and others simply by the touch and then eventually by the look. The resonance of how to do it will be picked up without saying anything. That's where you're at now.

You're moving into the power if you allow the human condition to understand this, the moving into the power, the heart chakra, which is a green healing energy. It heals anything. It doesn't have a problem. You're working that way now.

Psalm 6

On your Internet, you have this date that many are focusing on now: September 27, 28, tying it in with Hebrew traditions and other traditions, the fourth-blood-moon thing, Wiccan traditions. There is a stabilization factor that is being put in place to slow this down a bit. We always try to slow it down. Hopefully, things will pick up and make it through. But this time we're having difficulty slowing this one down, this movement. You have Nibiru coming into your system, creating an influence within your magnetic fields on all planets. It affects consciousness.

These are not the gods. These are entities from the past. Yet they are entities that are still present because their orbit is so far different from yours. Some of your beings in your politics have aligned themselves with some very negative forces purposefully because they think in their own minds a certain cleansing is needed, but it's not the appropriate cleansing. So you're in that, and that's why your politicians now all over your world are having troubles and difficulties with their people. People are beginning to wake up, as you say, in their own selves. These are the changes that are occurring.

You're in six weeks of intense emotional understanding. You have noticed daily the energies have changed. You have noticed the day feels different. You are feeling the effect of the space shifting. People are becoming more pleasant as the space shifts because it's pleasant space that's shifting. They just have a feeling to act differently. It's going to occur more and more. This helps stabilize this region, particularly your Arizona, right now. This is a borderline safe place, so to speak. You have a tremendous amount of energy coming from the East and a tremendous amount of energy coming from the West, and it's stabilizing itself at the borders of Arizona.

Why? It's not necessary to explain that at the present time. You are making a connection with your spiritual ancestors who are protecting the space for you. Hopefully you will wake up like your grandfathers and your grandmothers and those ancient ones to understand the significance of these times. They are protecting the space for you because the human condition doesn't know how to do it yet — so thankfulness is there in that realm. This is where you thank the angels and pray for the angels and help with prayers. Prayers are important.

The most important prayer from our perspective for the human condition, individually, is Psalm 6 because it asked for repentance at the beginning, and it asks for the enemies of your self, not just in the physical construct, all levels. Time is a direction — up. Psalm 6 asks for your enemies to be ashamed suddenly because shame is the deterrent for these beings, not pain, not pain, because everyone recognizes them for who they truly are when the shame hits, and they do themselves too. This is what is occurring.

The Many Mansions of God

Do you have a question?

You said in the first knowledge of incarnation there is a limitation occurring in the placement of the planets in the [astrological] house. Is that a way, then, that our natural abilities are limited?

Yes, it also assisted.

It also assisted, ah!

It increased.

That was the most important one. So as we wake up to our natural selves now, how will those limitations be released?

What you will begin to understand is the significance of Jupiter in your chart, its place. That's the first one, and everyone usually focuses on Venus and Uranus for the excitement and all that. But the next one you should check is Mars because that's where your conflicts are and in the house there.

In the house but not the sign? The house is more important than the sign, hmm.

Well, the sign is your influence, yes. But the house gives you a more … it's your house, see …

I see. It's where I live, and it relates to me. Ah, okay.

Yeah and it relates to all of your lineage too because that is where you get the wisdom and coming to choose those houses. You came in to assist here. You chose the wisdom of the house and placed it there so that you would be reminded, basically.

Well, that's the part that I asked for clarification, but the rest of it is so awesome that if we can only live through it, I guess ...

Well, this is the symbolism of the many mansions of God. Each house is a mansion.

Oh, okay.

You all have twelve mansions, actually thirteen, but that's another story.

When will we know about the thirteenth one?

When you find out who you are. You're the thirteenth mansion.

Okay, I don't want to interfere with the energies, so we're good.

That's how that works, primarily. Now we're working for health, the idea of health — remove a pain from the body and remove unnecessary conditions that no longer provide service. That's how health is achieved. The understanding now is that it's in the space. Health is in the space.

Can you amplify on that?

Your peach is healthy. The thought of the peach when you ate the peach, what did it take you back to?

Oh, just back to pure delight — absolute delight.

Did you have childhood memories come back?

No.

Or the last time you ate the peach, that sort of thing? A flash of visions of a tree?

No, none of that.

Contemplate it next time.

Okay, I will.

When you eat the peach, thank the peach.

I did. Best peach I ever ate.

Then you get that the construct, the peach, actually knew it was for you. I know you just think you get these things, but the peach knew it was coming to you. That needs to be understood.

That's weird because I never buy fruit at Sam's Club, but they had a sample, and I said, "Give me more!"

Something called you; the peach called you. So this is your connection with the natural things, you see. And peach is the color that you're going to start seeing in your sky too, by the way.

Who are those ... ?

They are angelics; they are angels.

I am trying to lead with stuff without distracting.

Yes, yes. I am bringing it up because you are doing it. You just don't realize that the peach called you.

All right, wonderful.

You think it was you who desired the peach. The peach gave you the desire because it wanted to communicate with you, that kind of thinking.

It's how we need to think?

Yeah. That provides the health to the body. If you listen to the foods calling you in a proper way (how say you?), some foods, you know, are not appropriate, and you'll feel a call there, but it's not the food that's calling you there. It's another being pushing that food. There is a difference. There is a requirement that the body knows and answers the call, but there is a desire there that pushed at you that is not yours. Those are very subtle lines of professorship, I guess you'd call it, perfection of self.

You have explained how the coffee bean wants to experience. But are there other beings pushing their desires on you, or is it the substance itself?

Oh yes. Yes, sometimes it's the substance itself in what you call the healing mode capacity. Other times, it's other beings wanting to get into the body when you have that sip. You just have to identify it. Then once a being comes in the body, you introduce yourself, and say, "Oh, I get it. No problem, thank you very much. You can leave."

All of these plants have intelligence, but the human condition hasn't respected the plant, and that's why you're having difficulty now. You are aware of these GMO foods and everything. It's a concept that is taking control of foods here. That's why they poisoned the river. These foods coming are going to be dangerous. There's a control function going on here for what people have available for themselves as a way to perpetuate their own consciousnesses without the influence of others forcing it. They are trying to force it through the foods. You already messed up your corn. So you're going to figure your selves out here.

The primary thing to really be considered is thankfulness for the water because the water will lead you, really. You can be inspired by the water, literally. It will give you clarity of thought and clarity within the systems. When you drink your water, as you drink it, think of your heart being purified, just washed. Whatever is there, it just washes it like a shower as it goes in the body, and you'll feel it release through the chakras.

CHAPTER

8

The Cosmic Shock in September: the Mind and the Brain

August 25, 2015

We are going through this phase in your August preparing for your September. You have an innocence in the essence of your self. Within that innocence is knowing, and sometimes that knowing of the innocence leads to an arrogance of the innocence. This is the process you are in now. Your month of September is going to even this out. It is going to show you the power of your innocence, and it's also going to show you the arrogance of the self within that innocence. So it's the arrogance that is going to be, we're going to say, figured out within the self and modified in a way that becomes knowledge, not arrogance. Arrogance is a false receptacle for your ideas that are not yours, actually.

So you are going through this process of understanding your structure — bones, flesh, skin, sinew, and things. Now you're going into the feeling part of your self. Within the solar plexus, within the heart chakra, within the root, and within the naval — with all the chakras — they're feeling energy in there. Your training and comfort is coming to you as you move from chakra to chakra within your system of self, gently out. Now, within this expansion of consciousness that you are going through, there is this concept of death; the heavy fear, the death thing. But life is always life, no matter when life is living.

The circumstances surrounding the living quality, however, is determined by the processing of your own eternal energies in what is termed the continuity of consciousness of self within the environment that you are in. You term them memories. "This is how I react in 'this' situation and 'this' sort of thing," and you turn it to your mind. But your mind, in the human condition in your processes of spirit and body, is behind you. That's what you've done. That's why the mind knows it. The brain, the physical brain in the skull, is what is present. The brain is present. The mind is behind you. You have no mind in your future yet because you haven't done anything. So you have no accomplishment that the mind understands.

The brain synapses are power and movement. That's what you're going through now. That's why people are having all the reflections in their lives: past mistakes, wish they had done some things, and glad they did these things that have passed. That's the mind. Now, in order to know something, to know the knowledge of it in the present, requires the brain. Perception — the feelings, the sights, the reaction — to things interiorly, you see a thing, and it changes because you've noticed. The brain is used for the present moment. The mind is what your history is. So when you find out you don't have a mind, which is a process for spiritual forces through your brain, your presence is always now. It's not worried about what you did in the past or what could possibly be in the future because you're basing the future on what your mind has done in the past. It is not pertinent to what your new future is going to be.

You're going to learn to breathe with your brain. And by breathing, I mean interpreting, the interpretive function within the soul processes of the heart chakra. You have already learned what not to do. How do you know that look back in your mind? You will find out what you shouldn't do again. That's how you know. As you go forward, you are always correcting yourselves in a process for the dignity of self. That's all, not the overlording of anyone. Yet you are going through this overlording thing where this war consciousness and conquering thing is coming strong because that is the fear, losing something that was not yours in the first place.

The beings who are doing this war thing are sending others to kill, and they are having no part of it. They don't want to stop it; there's too much money to be made, the money thing. Yet when that goes away, the money thing, you have a whole other issue, and your issue is going to be food and water. You've had this process in your consciousness now, say, food for months, and you're going to go into survival mode entities because you haven't been paying attention to your teachers' teachers.

The Ball of Light

You haven't been paying attention to anything; you haven't even studied with the self. You haven't. Your United States of America is sleepy. You have everything here, pretty much, compared to other countries in which the babies can't even get food. You can't even get food for some in your own country. You have your immigration problems with people coming across your borders and things like that. Water flows, consciousness flows, humans who are involved with consciousness flow in a civilized understanding of spiritual wisdom that there should be no borders. Your structure is so isolated that people are in their apartments or in their houses and there's no communal activity — unless you're working the government's understanding, and that's the wrong understanding.

You're seeing what's happening: the power grabs and things, special privileges for some and not for others. So the ability to walk freely as a human on the planet is not available. Yet when you were born, you thought it was that way. It is going to become that way. Those who have the ability to walk and be with knowledge are going to be those who walk and have the ability with knowledge.

When this light hits it — I am going to say "hits," just expresses itself — it doesn't have to go anywhere. It's already there. What it does is call like-minded consciousness together in the spiritual sense. It brings it together in unification and says one word, "Om," and everyone will vibrate to that energy somewhere. In your world, meaning your Earth here, there are many countries already hearing the sound from the invisible — not coming from any machine or anyone singing it. You can hear the hums, we'll call it, the cosmic hums. That's the approach; there's a being coming, literally. As he moves, the sound precedes him. He pushes it; it's there just to let everyone know he's coming so that everyone won't be surprised.

The first indication you are going to receive that this is a presence after the sound will be a foot. You're going to see a foot, just a foot — just a foot — and that's all you will need to see. That should create the understanding that there's one watching and participating in this next movement of spiritual consciousness occurring here. That's why you're having these wars, the argument about God all over, all over, all over — religion to religion to religion:

"I'm more right than you are."

"No, you're not."

"Yes, I am," all of this.

But is anybody doing anything to cease conflict? How are you going to cease conflict? Well, you have to stop the bullets. You just make the ammunition inoperable, and then you shake the planet to get attention somewhere else. Then the struggle for survival becomes more paramount than the killing for space.

You have definite problems in the leadership of all your countries. Each one has difficulty in the understanding of the sacredness of the human condition within the consciousness and responsibility of the particular country you are in. The whole thing has been convoluted, and you know it. There is no one being you can go to now. It's going to have to be, what is termed, God, who is everywhere, and you put a name on it, if it makes you feel comfortable, because that is your own defiance.

You know you came from somewhere, humans, and you know you're going somewhere; you're always going to be somewhere. The understanding in the teachings is a process called breath, thankfulness for it, and the water. Breath and water are your new two secrets, and they should be your best companions. Breath should be your most favorite lover and companion because you can't succeed too long without it, and water is next. Then you have an understanding of what is termed your elemental kingdoms: When you respect them, they respect you, and communication becomes rapid. The elementals know you, and they understand as you approach. There is a whole new change going on.

Now, just because there are spiritual conditions within the elementals doesn't mean they don't have attitudes, because they certainly do. That is how the human condition has learned to develop its own attitudes to certain things: from the elementals, because they are firm in their attitudes. They have applied them for centuries. The human condition hasn't understood that yet throws it around.

You have systems of health that are required here for the bodies to continue to be alive. You have your doctors and surgeons and medical professions. What if you didn't? What if you didn't have them? You can think back, "Well, I would've been dead back there, but I had a doctor." Each one is because you know what you should not have done that caused the condition. You do know it. The condition to health and understanding is much more refined than the condition to death and not understanding — arguing, arguing, and arguing.

The law of attraction is really governed by innocence, governed by innocence. The law within the innocence has a perversion in a way; it doesn't want to be innocent anymore because it looks as if everyone else is having more fun. It's called the condition of doing whatever you want. Yet the repercussions are within the health system of the body. The spiritual force does not want to be in the body that is *not* aligned unto the function of life, which is called breath and water — the perpetuation of the understanding of breath.

When you get the understanding of breath correctly, then your vision changes. Instead of being inside the body looking out and perceiving and receiving, you will be inside the body preparing yourself to receive your next manifestation. You will see it, and it will be there because you called it forth, not seeing to look for it. There's a difference. Seeing it there because you called it forth, you just have to look in the right direction, the right direction. Time is a direction, and it is up. You're bringing it down to yourself in front of you. That hasn't happened yet. Your mind hasn't had this experience yet because it's behind you. It is not caught up to where your brain is now. It hasn't. It can never do it. It will always be behind you.

That is the significance of your astrological chart's tipping. It comes horizontal with your waist like the Adam Kadmon so that you know where you are, which house, and the breath continues.

That is another story because you are involved — once that horoscope tips from the back here, literally — in communication with the planetary systems that are there, like a telephone. You just have to touch it. You have a dialing number there. Then it spins, and you can spin it, but you don't want to spin it right away. Just leave it where it is until you figure out how it works. But you can touch the planets like a telephone, really, in that body. But that's not the point right now. The point right now is to understand that you are going to need the breath, peace, safety, and water as you go through this cosmic shock, I will call it, in your September.

The Cosmic Shock in September

This cosmic energy coming now has force. It has feeling, and what you are feeling in the heaviness now is "its" feeling. It's just gently, like this, coming [expression of hands opening small], yet there's more coming, so you have to understand this portion.

In a manner, you have this force that has a great desire to replicate itself through anything — trees, plants, humans, animals, insects, all creatures, birds. It has an intense desire to, you call it, create. Some beings like the name Creator. But the process of creation is difficult to understand, and that's why you're here in the human condition: to understand what creation is and the results of it. You are seeing the results of some creations now, several actually, and the original spontaneous I Am One declaration that knew it before anyone else desired to share it equally.

It has no "better than you" clause in its vocabulary. It doesn't even have a vocabulary. It just creates. Yet it has established laws, and by that I mean boundaries, so that one planet doesn't go smashing into another planet. They maintain orbit: The stars stay where they are, and the ants crawl around the way they are supposed to.

The only condition that is not working appropriately in this great creation scheme is the human condition.

It devises killing devices for everything. Poison plants, kill them. Bullets for humans to kill anything; the whole design structure is wrong. In the function of it, you want to get rid of what does not agree with you and your space. The human condition does not know how to live appropriately among other things. It doesn't. It's saying an animal should live "this" way; a bird should live "this" way. Birds know how to fly; they even know who's flying them. Animals know how to walk; they even know who's walking them.

The human condition is the only one who doesn't know who's walking them or what they're doing unless someone tells them to do it. Your structure, this is what you do. The freedom of the ability to think and program or establish a mind consciousness where you have foundation — that's what the mind is for, a foundation — and proceed from there. That's why you have pyramids, for your instruction, basically: its foundation, all of this, to go to the top where it's clear. That's where the brain is. Except you can move; you're a pyramidal energy that can move, and you have functions in a manner to reaffirm the nature of peace within space. That's what your job is, to walk as gods here, not to overrule and overlord everyone. Animals already know you're god. If they're reacting differently to you, then you don't know that you are, but they know.

The human condition tries to force the will on the natural kingdom, but you can't. You have to become more natural and move within that. The perfection of nature understands God walking, understands God between the trees. That's why they are so alert and are aware of it. The only condition is the human condition because you have been influenced by Satan and doubt, one of his greatest weapons, I guess, his teaser toys that he uses. He is working through a lot now with his ridicule of the human condition. So in your allegorical story, throw it in the face of God. That is going to change, and the human condition now is going through those changes.

Your month of September is going to be quite interesting. Many of the spiritual teachers are trying to calm the energy down, trying to just modify it a little bit. You're not going to change a lot of it, but you will try to modify it so that things don't happen. We're even trying to change the orbit of the planet just a bit so that this thing misses. Just move it; that's all you have to do.

But consciousness here is calling it, and you have some very great difficulties in the spiritual tradition. I don't care which one you pick. Under your United States stuff going on here in this country you are becoming, I think you have crossed the border as far as the Sodom and Gomorrah thing. It appears that way. It appears there is going to be validation of that soon. You just can't continue in this direction in a responsible consciousness in a way that can be understood and pleasant to all.

All humans now are going through their own argumentative phase in the jurisdictional phase, and the suggestion now is to try to get back into the womb before you were born during your meditations. Don't worry about what's coming. You'll be shown that when it's appropriate. But get back into your womb before you "became." Try to remember the nature of your self within the seed. How did you get to be in the seed that swam to the egg? How? That was the development part right there. Then how were you the receptor of the egg and the seed? How did that happen? How? How? Bring your self back before, and learn the thought of your parents that taught you or that you answered to.

From the invisible realm, you answered to and accepted the

union. You were the union. You are the result of those two processes — the thought of the mother and the thought of the father. You are the result of it. Now, with your own brain energies, the alterations can be understood. That's what the importance of a brain is in being present. An understanding of the mind behind you has passed. It has passed. You have done that, and the result in the physical condition could be from the past, yes, but the brain is present. It can alter the current condition.

The mind has given you the establishment of a body; that's basically what it is, and you have gone through the social consciousness construct as a result of it. It was in the mind because that's what you have done, and know that the brain can present you a new future. The mind can give you a foundation that you can say, "Oh, I know how to do that," but the brain being present now can fix the mind, clean the corners of it, and each corner there should be a forgiveness because that's where you stuffed stuff, top to bottom.

So you can start forgiving yourself for your past and your present and your future because you are not going to have it correct. You get a little more correct each time, but you're not going to move on to perfection because you enjoy the confusion of it. The perfection is what you are looking to attain in the delicacy of the condition you call your selves. This is what is working now. It's the problematic function of life that keeps you alive. Is it just you wanting to be alive? No, because a lot of you just don't want to be here. But you don't know where you're going to go when you're dead. You've already done the dead thing; that's why you have a life now. So you are living in the understanding of the perpetuosity of what is termed the feeling of love within the body of self. You already know the construct, how to do that. The construct is your self.

The appreciation of the self is what is being accomplished

now. The unity of self. The dignity and worthiness of self is coming through now. This is the month you're going through in your September. It's really starting to take effect this week. It's the third week of August, and it will really build up and prepare you for the second week of September, and during the third week of September, you're moving into another energy.

So you're going through these forces now. It's not a galactic movement you are feeling but a cosmic force, now much stronger. It's in the energy of the sunlight, and the different rays coming that haven't been experienced here before are more intense. They excite or make nervous, I could say, the vibratory flags of recognition that exist within each chakra. Vibratory flags, those are the personality of each chakra. They recognize this frequency coming, and there's a tendency to be obedient to it because it will straighten you up.

That recognition will come with a sound that will go down the spine and be felt in the body and come out the hands. You will feel it. I want to say different entities, yet in the interpretation of the word "entities," there could be confusion. You are moving, I will say, into a different species besides the ignorance of the human condition. You are a human, yet you are going to become more specific within the human condition. You have categories in your society: you have doctors, you have shamans, you have police, you have judges, you have lawyers, and you have all of this. You're not going to need any of it because you are going to understand you are it.

The Seven Spirits of God and Their Levels

You are justice, which is under your auspices of Archangel Gabriel. He is truth; therefore he is justice. You are in those recognition patterns now that are being established according to those categories within self. You are going through what we would term the seven spirits of God, and the first one is love, and the last one is the fear of God and the understanding of it. In between are wisdom, knowledge, and understanding, all of those processes that will be felt by the acknowledged part of your self. It is going to feel it. And the acknowledged part of yourself is your bones and the muscles and the sinew that allow you to move the bones. Anything else is extra baggage until you understand the function of the organs and that the personality for each being in the organs came from the same seed.

The heart is a being. It's going to reincarnate as another part of you. You're training it. The liver, the lungs, these other entities are here to assist the heart in its knowledge gained and to prepare the heart with the ability to think correctly for its next incarnation as a physical form, where it will have a heart to train. You're the personality training these functions.

Each beat of your heart is a training form for an entity not physical. It's the auric field of the heart itself. Those who are going to desire to have a body of their own with their own heart, lungs, liver, and kidney are preparing themselves. This is what the Buddha one is doing here: preparing another incarnation of your selves. This is how it works. In one manner, you're on Earth searching for parents in your next lifetime. You are not aware of that, but you're on the lookout for it.

That's why many old people on their deathbeds enjoy the parents of youngsters, so the dying spirit could perhaps enter through the youngsters and get a body. Those are things you're hardly even aware of. Yet there is a function within certain churches that know that and do that in practice, this sort of interfering thing. They are working toward understanding this because you want to bring in proper spiritual forces.

You have many demonic beings trying to enter now — in anybody — just for the experience of it because there is going to be a change going on here. You see evil, and fortunately you do not have to have the expression of it in your wars in your physical locality. It is really hard to sleep at night when bombs are dropping. It creates a shift in consciousness in everyone there. Basically, then, nobody knows who is right or who is wrong. It is just that the bomb didn't get you. It doesn't have to happen here, yet there are beings who want to create that sort of circumstance now in your cities with these race wars they are trying to get going. There are many trying to stop the ignorance of it.

You are going through a realization process of a collective consciousness, but the realization of the outcome is not what you are expecting. The realization of this change will not be clear until after it's already completed because of the resistance to the understanding that Spirit is Spirit and God is God, and you are not it. Yet you're supposed to be, but that is not the occasion. That is happening this September.

You may have noticed in your month of August that each day seems to be getting heavier and heavier. I have said that before. I told you it's going to get heavier, so you're going to have to learn to keep the spine erect because you have a greater self of you who wants to talk to you, and the only way it can talk to you is when you are sort of out of the way. What happens with the human condition is you have a brain that has the ability to think, yet often you refer to the mind. When you do that, you call the mind forward. It overlaps your brain, and you're in the other process again.

So you have units of consciousness you need to put in position; tell them and the mind to settle down. Tell the heart to settle down. You have to tell the kidneys to stop doing that, and you start doing what is affecting the kidneys. Through all of this thing, you learn to communicate with the body forces of your self.

Someone Else Is Going to Need You

You have an understanding so that you can be present when someone else needs you. That is what is going to happen. You're going to need to be present because someone else is going to need you, because you know the person doesn't know what is happening. That feeling will be there, and then say, "Peace to all beings," and stabilize because you are going to be talking to spiritual forces now, not human. Humans have no idea what is really happening, unless you are talking about the price of gas and maybe the cost of food or that you should be eating "this" and eating "that." That knowledge should already be known at least twenty or thirty years ago about proper food and diet. But in the human condition, there's arrogance or justification of things.

You are going through the concept of mind and knowing it didn't work and then what does work. You're setting the good stuff in your little silver boxes over "here" and the other stuff to get rid of over "here." You keep your little silver boxes ready for more. Soon you'll have to get rid of all that because you are going to realize that the breath providing you consciousness is all that there really is. It enjoys water and all of the other things. The being in the breath is a very tiny being, yet it can be everywhere at the same time. It doesn't have a problem with the function of when it is and always will be.

"When" is not its issue. It is always present. When the understanding is there for the brain, this little invisible being that is always present, you are going to learn something different about yourself first. Then it will develop a sense of safety second. Third, the knowledge base increases, and the heart starts beating differently. It has an "I know" beat, an "I Am" beat. It doesn't need permission from another being.

So you are going through an interesting position here, and you're having a lot of (how do you beings say?) contact with extraterrestrials, UFOs. But they're not UFOs. They are beings. They are primarily here to defend you from other forces outside of your world that you know nothing about and that have ulterior motives. You are not aware of who your true benefactors are yet, but you will be.

Exposure of Disrespect and the Ball of Light

You have some scientists and doctors joking and laughing about cutting heads off fetuses and implanting them somewhere, doing things like this inappropriately. It is a sickness now. All of this stuff is being exposed, and the disrespect and indignity to the human condition and the seeds of life are ridiculous here. It's not even, well, we know who is working that one. But it's in your environment and consciousness, so this is a separation that is going to happen.

There are those who are going to understand life and how to live it and breathe it and be with it when it happens. Then there are those who will not. They are not going to understand it, and they are simply going to fall. They will fall. They will fall down, literally, and not be able to get up. This September could be the month for that, a lot of it. The insanity has already started to happen. People are going around shooting people on trains, or trying to. When did this start to become popular entertainment? You have difficulties now, and the cleanup is going to be dramatic. It will be a dramatic cleanup. I understand it to be permanent when it happens. That's where you are at.

If this white ball of light hits your country as we have shown him [the channel], we are saying "if" now because we are trying to … we understand what judicial process is. And we understand the force and superiority of this authority coming, and it wants it known. We also understand the difference in being able to receive this much energy with the human condition, how many are going to be left, basically. So we are trying to get this thing modified. That is what prayers are for, to slow this down. Slow this down. There is a sense of urgency being built even within the spiritual realms of calm and grace. What is going to occur hasn't happened before, so they say. So nobody has a mind on this one. The present is your brain's process for the thankfulness of life, the fact that you have one, number one, and to make it through this.

October

This is the month, your October, when things should be a little clearer. You might have disturbances in your streets. There's another thing that's working there. Your country might not be your country as you think it is any longer.

Space is to be held, and be thankful that you even have space. Space is the grace. I have said that before. If you have space, you are under grace. You are within the grace because there are other things in the space, and you are not alone. That is what the clue is there. It is like a big wheel, and when space shifts, everyone shifts with it.

You are in your cubic function of the mind, which is six directions, and you're going beyond that, into an expansion of consciousness, which includes the cubic function of self — which is beyond the planets. It's how you knew to choose the planets before you got your astrological chart. You already knew you were in that school. You knew the function of each planet and how it worked, and then you came through with this agreement, which is inscribed on your chart in your back. You are living it.

The part of you that knew that is joining you now. It is proud of its accomplishments, actually. There are not many in those greater realms who desired to come down here to assist in this realm. Graduation is going to be quite exciting! I will put it this way: You're going to have more knowledge of your self in a sense that you have truly earned it! It's an accomplishment, that sense. It's a good feeling in the body.

Health to the body, mind, and spirit are working here now. Sometimes beings feel energy come to them, and they think it's one being, but it's really another being, a tagalong of beings. You have to be aware, in a manner, when you feel an influence. As you're receiving thought, try to pick up a name where that thought came from or whether its yours. Understand that your brain is present, and the mind is behind you. There is an important distinction here with these new concepts that are going to be realized and activated on. Remember the mind is behind, and the brain is present. It is developing a new capacity. This is where mind influences matter; in the front, it is present.

Are you saying specifically from the frontal cortex?

Yes. Once you can understand the mind is behind you and the brain is present, you can pull the energy of the mind forward. It will come up through here. You can use all powers, but do not expect the same results.

Oh, new results because you have new intent to understand. Say more about how it comes up.

You call it forth. It wants to volunteer information that as you move into the brain being present, influenced by the present, the old power of the mind is coming up so that now the mind has moved into wisdom. Then it works with the brain. The brain in the present moment determines things. It commands things and manifest things.

But you're above the river of social consciousness?

Yes, you can't remember what they are thinking about. You don't want to. You're actually in a canoe riding on it, and when you're in the canoe, you can look on the river and see the words going down. You can see that's going down "that" way. That's going down "that" way and over the other, to be saying that.

But you're not influenced?

No. Health to body, mind, and spirit. Strength to body, mind, and spirit. Peace to all beings. We are through.

CHAPTER

9

You Are in a New Presence Now, and Your Heart Begins to Speak

September 1, 2015

This is how it works — change; you're always in a state of change. You always are. The stability required for change to occur comfortably within the system of self is the knowledge of safety and comfort, or the sense of it, of safety.

The human condition is going through the process now of living through the seven spirits of God, and there is a different pronunciation at each level. The first level, the invisible one (the first one), is love, and then you have wisdom, understanding, and knowledge. The one you're working on now that the human condition is going through is the seventh one. That seventh spirit is the old fear-of-God thing. Now, in that understanding of the fear of God — it is more like the respect for it, respect for the enormous power there, because misappropriation and application of it can damage you. It's like watching a child playing with matches. It's fun to see the flame; the child drops the match, and it burns the house down. It is the same sort of thing with the fear thing.

You have to have respect to handle this next idea of your self, you see, because the idea of your self was not known to you for this framework in the womb. Your idea of yourself in the womb was where you came from — past-life things. You had a connection with your previous mind; you were sensing your previous mind, what you knew as your mind. What you knew was how to think, actually, the process. It wasn't the words; the words are just manifestations of energy forces for communication in the physical world. Each country has different words for the same thing, but they don't even mean the same thing when you say them. It is a different influence.

Each consciousness of a country is different, yet you are all conscious as humans, and that working is the process you are going through: One country is better than another. "This" country is better than "that." You are doing it with your religions, and all you are doing is fighting. You don't understand why the uniqueness of your community or country is there. It's unique for a reason. Each country has consciousness and verbal speech. It has emotional context and influences that if understood correctly within the environment of growing up there, you would have the understanding of it.

The Completion

Well, your planet now is moving to *another* level of consciousness where it is going to be *planetary* consciousness, so you are all going to communicate the same way — not in the same language; I didn't say that. You're going to communicate in the *same way*. You're going to understand telepathy and the interpretation of it. You will pick up a thought and have an emotional construct in your body, and you will feel the energy of it. You will convert it to words so that you can play with it. You're going to go through the experience of emotional empathy with everything. Now, just as beings can influence another's thought telepathically — and those are demonstrated by hypnosis — so too there is this emotional language. Empathy, you beings call it, but it is much more than that. There is a feeling energy that floats in the air without a word.

That's why sometimes beings feel this oppression, density, and heaviness coming, because you're getting communication from the astral, from the invisibles. But they do not communicate verbally; they communicate emotionally and visually. They prefer visually because the visual (with the eyes), when you see, your whole system has a reaction. There is a chemical adjustment for the interpretation, for judgment, and for everything. That's the next step, but we have to get the human condition through its emotional confusion. You are like a bunch of babies in a crib crying, screaming, "I want this!" or "I want that!" or "Mine! Mine! Mine!" You don't understand that there is a unit — by unit, I mean this world, your planetary world system, your walk-upon ball that you are here with, and the beings within it and everything.

In the current human condition, there has been such a development of selfishness that it is unbelievable. We are surprised that anything is alive. The animals now are starting to adjust. They understand the compassionate nature that's coming for the development of the human condition, the next one, the next level of development. You are going to shift, you're going to understand priorities, and it's going to be food and water. You are going to look at yourself for what you haven't done and decide you must do something because you are walking on a path here called the Completion. It is called the Completion. This portion of the time frame in the physical world is a door that opens access to understanding what you are doing here, why you are here, how you got here, and the purposeful intent of your self for the self.

The self is your body, your bones. You are going to figure out the importance and the significance of your bones. Now, once you have that concept understood, then you begin replicating, healing the self within the self, the physical structure. Then you begin to enjoy yourself. In other words, you are sitting in one place in your room, and there's a chair across from you. Nobody is in it, so you just simply *perform* yourself to go to the chair without getting up and walking. So you will see yourself sitting in the other chair.

Invisibles in the Astral

This is an exercise with the astral and the emotional bodies. The other part is that the anchor part is your bones, and they aren't going to move *unless you know how to disappear them and get them to the chair without walking to it* and then reappear them. Once you understand that significant tone there, and there is also a color involved, that is the manifestation of you in the "in and out" of you, because you blink on and off continually out of here, whether you know it or not. Once you understand those processes, then you have a whole new commitment to the life force that is available here, because then the requirement comes to teach others how to do it. So there is a sustainable system.

This is what is going to cause the … well, because of the construct of the human condition and its thought processes and what it does with its mind, it doesn't know anything. It only knows once it's done something, and then it thinks that's it, but that's back there [points behind his head]. The mind is behind the head. The brain is in the present. Your brain, in the consciousness of your self with breath, is in the present. The life force is in the breath, and you are a chemical reaction because when you breathe out, you are exchanging chemicals to the system that you no longer need but that others perhaps do.

The Holy Spirit Is Breathing You

We have said this before: You are living your death. You understand how to die within the consciousness without the fear of it and how to live with the breath and the thought of it and the thankfulness too, because that is what is going to have to be understood here. There is a thankfulness in the fact that you can breathe.

There is another force, which is the Holy Spirit, who is coming. Well, it's already here. It is starting to breathe through beings. You take a breath, but that wasn't you. That was a portion of you leaving and the Holy Spirit giving you a blessing. When people are feeling they must clean house, as you are in your cleaning, there is an inspiration there to do it. That was inspired by the Holy Spirit because it is inspiring cleaning and knowing the preparation of what is coming, you see. When you clean your house or your environment, you think you are cleaning the exterior portion, but you're really cleaning your interior portion. The interior portion is getting cleaned because those are the old ideas that are sticking to the walls.

Everything is coming down, and there is a whole new thing. There is a vibratory frequency arriving that enjoys cleanliness. It just won't be around disturbing forces. When it appears in the human condition — and it is going to appear — it's going to knock down walking humans. It will. It will be like you walking into a clear, blank wall. You won't even know it's there, and you will fall right down because it has substance and power. It is a force, and it doesn't need to manifest itself as a human to prove its force. All it has to do is basically just shift space sideways. You will get dizzy and won't know what happened. It doesn't even have to be an earthquake. Nature is changing, and your weather's changing. You are seeing that.

The Emotional Understanding of Your Thoughts

The relationship now between the weather and your thoughts still hasn't been understood. You are in your "manipulation of weather" thing with your machines. You haven't the understanding here that during the day your Sun in the sky receives your thoughts. There is a being, a spiritual force there, that receives your thoughts. Then when the Moon comes, it reflects the light of the Sun to you, and you experience the emotional understanding of the thoughts that you had sent to the Sun that day. You are not aware of that cycle. That is how it works.

Because you are 60 percent [60 percent for adults and 70 percent for children] water in your system, or close to that, you are influenced by the Moon, in a way. Now, the water oceans of your Earth call the Moon and push the Moon away. It is not the Moon that causes the high tides. It is the rotation of the planet and the ocean moving itself. And it will push the Moon, and it will pull the Moon. There is a whole other energy thing there.

In that pushing and pulling, the same thing is going on in your inner fluid body. You all have desires, and you all get angry because they haven't been fulfilled, but you forgot the communication process, the delays, and the timing of your birth. There is significance in the time of your birth, not just the date, now. I have already mentioned the date. And the resonance in your bones, that should've come up. In the time of your birth, there is a note there. When you get your numbers together, there is a musical note like a bell that rings it's time for class. You receive that note; you had a knowledge of an opportunity to proceed from the other mind, from your old mind.

Prayer of the Bones

Now, the new mind that is developing is the one that understands the forgiveness of self and stepping forward. Your legs go in front of you when you walk. What you have not become aware of is that there are prayers in your shins and in your toes that pray for you as you step, and you have no clue. It is a signature of your self, so when you walk, you're praying, but you forgot the prayer. You don't know what it is, so there is a confidence in it because the bones have taken care of it.

The depictions of these symbols are in your Keys of Enoch. It shows you the thing. It's not written what the prayer is, but it shows you the glyph of it. When you understand that your legs, as you go forward, are praying for you so that you are safe where you are going, then the heart chakra begins to understand itself, and it communicates inwardly with the physical. The physical is the bones — the flesh and skin. The muscles are much less physical than the bones, which are crystalline structures that have harmonics, and the blood is formed there. It is formed by, we are going to call it, the caress of the Holy Spirit, but it really is the kiss of the Holy Spirit. The blessing of the bones forms your blood, and you are in the process of self.

The blood of you is really you; it holds the thoughts and the desires and runs through the system. *What you are not aware of is your heart, your physical heart, is the next incarnating personality you are going to have when you choose your incarnation. You are training your heart for your next system with the knowledge of it.* It has the four muscles, and in the juncture is the secret cave where the light of you resides, and this electrical thing pumps it. Your Buddha one sits in the solar plexus, here in the soul area.

The heart desires to be in the body because that's all it knows. The soul does not want to be in the body. It wants to be out and be free. So you are working with your soul and your heart now, but now the next level is that you're going to know, you will soon, that your soul is training your heart for a physical incarnation as a representation of the human condition. It will look like you, similar. The physical heart is going to be the next process of your mind. It's not the mind, but it's the love and desire to continue the four-beat thing. Each beat is one of the letters of YHWH, by the way. You are walking in that path of self, and development and construction, building your "self body" continually, so you know what you are doing.

Soon some (not all) are not going to have to incarnate through the womb to be physical anymore. You have learned that part, or should have, and now you're going from bone to bone where you are in this position, time, date, and space. Contemplation — you won't need a machine to do it. You shift. You have trained your brain. Your brain understands it, and you are in another time and space. You will be able to do that in your physical world now.

Say you are in your position in Flagstaff, Arizona, and you desire to be in a position in Phoenix. You just decide it and do it. You will know how to do it. You know what you're doing. You have a reason to be there, and then you come back. There has to be a purpose, not just to play. So the movement is the development of the — these are words that you beings played with, so we have to use them so that you will have a similar understanding — higher aspect of your self. You say it's your higher self, well, the desired self. You are your high self confused. The human condition is in an argument phase with and about God.

The meditation of the breath — God is within you and is within everyone. Then you go through the competition of the greater God thing. Then you got yourself caught into the money thing. You can't live without money. Well, you are proving yourself correct.

When you run out of money, you think you're going to die. But that's not the process. When you run out of breath, you die. When you run out of breath and water, then you understand prayer. Then you really understand what the significance of, what you call, the desert is because there is a secret there that calls for intense inner reflection and petitions because the one within you knows what it is doing. The heart is the child of your self for your next life, and it is going to need to be transformed. You are going to have to do the transformation now.

The physical process of being physical and staying physical, the use of physical to be physical, is coming to an end. You're going to need the use of spirit to be physical. You're going to understand the next step. The first step is, "What does sacred mean?" You'll get that eventually. The next step is, "What does holy mean?" In the human condition, you have in between you the metaphysical understanding, which is a bunch of words. So the constructs can at least form around something. But you had a presence before you were born, and that is what you need to get to. That presence that was there before you were born, that's in the solar plexus. That's what is working now or inclined to.

It'll be a little bit easier to have direct communication with the heart. Your bones want to embrace the heart, but they can't. The heart is gentle and has a significance in its beat. When you understand the significance of your heart just beating, then you get a relationship between the beat of your heart and the process in your brain — not the mind — the process in your brain when the heart beats. You'll find there are synapses in different sides of your brain. The left and right sides of the brain communicate with different auricles and ventricles of the heart at different times.

So you take a unification process of unifying the brain with lavender light; we have done this before. You sew the halves together, and this becomes lavender. Then you are breathing the lavender frequency, which is a representation of the Christ lavender robe. You have the healing self — all these things the masters came to teach so that they could be replicated (not repeated as blah, blah, blah) by you within the body system, replicated within the body.

Battle for Global Consciousness Supremacy

Prayers are important. Everybody knows what the word "prayer" means. It means a prayer. It can be any prayer that is still prayer, but the significance of the prayer is *how* you pray it and *what are you working with* when you pray it. In the human condition and your consciousness called America, or United States, you have your words for prayers. Well, each letter itself in the prayer is a prayer, is a being. You have to realize that when you say it. That's why the monks in your Tibetan tradition say, "Om," and each chakra is doing a thing. You have been confused by one, and you're coming out of that confusion now because there is going to be a recognition of the worthiness of your self.

You're going to get over the government thing because it's not keeping you alive. No, it's not. Governments are confusing you — all of them are. You have a battle going on now in consciousness for supremacy of the global consciousness in your world.

Countries and your leaders are looking to be in the supreme thing. It is not going to be pleasant; I'm going to say that. Prayer will get you through this. You have a condition developing now, and by the time you read this, you're going to see, literally, the insanity that's running your country and the globe, from corporations to Congress and all the other kingdoms running people's lives when people don't know what to do with their own. You're going to see the insanity of it, and when you see the insanity of it, you will recognize that you don't want to get caught in it. You don't want to get caught in it.

Do not pick sides on this one. Pick your own side, breathe, have clean water, and pray when this force begins to adjust itself. I want to call it "adjust itself" because it's already here; all it has to do is shift a little bit. Everyone is going to feel it at the same time. Everyone will feel it. Then you'll have a recognition of the sanctity of yourself. Some beings will pray, some will bow, and some will do nothing but lie down. This is the experience that is coming.

You've already seen in your skies the representation of lights flashing, and you have had these extraterrestrial experiences. You have heard the stories that some of these extraterrestrials have bred the soul out of the body, and now they are coming back because they found out that they need the soul in the system of self as this galactic force shifts itself, because everything is going at the same time, planets included.

You Are Going through an Opening Now

There is this knowledge-based entity that knows all things, and it's going to bring them all to a completion where ones are free, the ones who have earned the understanding of what freedom is, and that means you allow other beings their freedom. So you are in this place now where you're getting confirmation of the spiritual influence that surrounds you all the time, trying to guide you in the proper functioning of your life for a reason. You have guests coming, and they are a special type of guest. They are the healing ones. They don't even have to touch you to heal you. They simply have to be in your presence, and you are healed because you will vibrate to their frequency in the recognition and thankfulness of it, you see.

So the story has been told and told and told and told and told, and you're going to live the part of it now of the expectation of it. After the telling, there is an opening, and you're going through that now.

Human consciousness has the desire for death to be out of the body, but it doesn't know where it's going to go yet. It is not to do that. It is to stay in the body and reclaim your own territory, which is your body. Allow it to be healed and understand the presence of yourself because you have something else to do. That something else is to be available for others who don't have an understanding. You just hold the space; they will feel it. You're going through the emotional empathy, not telepathy, but emotional, and you will feel it. Everybody is feeling it. Then you just need to calm it.

The brains will fire, and by that I mean all the synapses will go off at the same time. A lot of people won't be able to handle that, and they will think they are required to talk. No. Enjoy the health that is coming to the body. This concept of talking is unpleasant at times because of the immature understanding of the value of words. Even the chakras are opening differently now. As the chakras open, the entities within the chakras express. It's just an expression. It's not a word. It's sung as a song. As they open and express, it affects the space, and some beings will develop a sense of shame that they haven't been prepared — without anybody saying anything. It will just come over them. It is the shame that defeats the demons.

That's the importance of Psalm 6, verse 10. It allows your enemies to be ashamed. It doesn't mean in the physical, though it will affect the physical, but it is also those you are not aware of who are influencing you in a negative way. They are ashamed, and then they stop because the shame thing has a way of taking away any power that they have had. So what we're trying to do, or actually are doing, is to build within each one that understands these messages a fort, towers, where you can hide, where you can sit and watch so that you are protected from the shame that is going to hit. So you build yourself a fortress; each fortress has four corners, and each corner has a prayer. You might not know what it is now. You haven't said it, but part of your system of self has already set it up for you.

Your Cube of Space Is Shifting

You have to remember there are six directions — north, south, east, west, top, bottom. You're in the middle of the cube within those six directions. The cube is your space, and the space is what is going to shift around the cube, and your cube will be in whatever space is shifting from the being that you are part of. You are a being, actually a sphere within a cube of another being, which is your self, and all of its worlds, in all of its worlds. You have doorways from world to world to world that you can walk through and receive information. This is the next understanding here as we go.

This process is what you are in now, and you are going to be allowed to understand the transformation of the body in time. You are in time, and time is a direction. It is up. The transformation of the body is you. You sleep to rejuvenate the body; that is the purpose of sleep. You know you're tired, so you go to bed, but the body is being rebuilt. You go through these desires and fantasies as you sleep, and you're working your old mind.

But as your new presence begins to develop, you will understand that the stars you see in your night sky are in the back of your head. You see them from a mirror reflected from a portion in a way, upward, memory, because you came from the stars, beyond them actually. You are attracted by the beauty and brilliance of all the lights they have around this system. You came in — some fell, some came in, and some were sent — and as you crossed through the (I have to use your terms) sidereal force to the earth force, where the astrological energy bends, you forgot as you became closer to the physical manifestation. The forgetting is part of your forgiving yourself because if you had returned with the memories of what your inappropriate behavior did to others (in previous incarnations), you would not be in any condition to perform any new duties. So forgetting was your forgiving.

Now you're in the same thing in the breathing portion of your self. If somebody has injured you or something, forget it. That will be the forgiving. Otherwise, you will be carrying it around all the time, wanting vengeance and this, that, and the other. This is what is going on. You're also seeing that there are no more secrets available. Everything is being exposed. All the nonsense and ridiculousness is being exposed.

The Being Life: You have ten steps to reclaim yourself, only ten, the golden marble steps —gold energy around but clear marble as you walk up them — like a Jacob's ladder thing. It's through the chakras, seven of them anywhere there, but the steps are labeled. Each step is one of the Ten Commandments. They are there for a reason, so you don't do damage to the self that is pure within the self, the pure self of yourself. That is the reason they are there, because they were given to perform a service of dignity for those who understood the true purpose of life, what life is.

There is a being — one being, one, only one — that provides life for all things. He *is* the life of all things. He *is in* the life of all things. He knows the life of all things. It is Life itself. He is everywhere and everywhen, in every unit of consciousness that is thinkable — and unthinkable, actually. It is a movement of preciousness and holiness.

The Beings Amen: You go from holy, then to holy, holy, and then you go to holy, holy, holy. There are three holies. And as you are working through the world of prayer, you'll understand what Amen means. There are seven of them; they are beings. They are beings. They are beings — personalities, very large personalities. When the human being says Amen, the spiritual being itself, standing by the throne, feels it. He looks (and I am putting this simplistically), he looks, he sees who is saying it, understands it, and turns back toward the throne. He will either say it, repeat it, or vibrate it. He will do something. Whatever his flavor is in the sincerity of the Amen, it gets replicated.

It's like a crystal. Well, he isn't a crystal. He is a movable being. He puts an energy to it and broadcasts it out. It will resonate to it. It passes the message on, you see. It passes the message on. So you have an Amen for your root chakra, you have an Amen for your naval chakra, you have an Amen for your solar plexus chakra, you have an Amen for your heart chakra, you have an Amen for your throat chakra, and you have an Amen for your sixth seal and crown the same. Then you become it, that vibratory thing, when all seven chakras understand the Amens. There is an amplification that happens. And you are transported to the presence of the Amens — not to the throne, but around it — and you get a different robe, a different color, and a different acknowledgment and things. Then you come back and the obligation, then, is to assist others in understanding these things, not for the pleasures of self, but for the pleasure of the understanding of the continuity of existence, no matter where you are or when. The importance now is to understand you are living through your death. That's what is important.

Your Breaths Are Numbered

You die daily with the words you think and say, and you don't have any idea yet what you have to do with all those words. The human condition is only allowed a certain number of breaths. Your breaths are numbered; your breaths are numbered. When you waste your breath with meaningless words, you limit your lifespan. That's not understood yet. The frequencies have been so convoluted. I will say that. You're beginning to find out that those who speak a lot have nothing to say. You can't even remember what they said. It's all a performance.

One of the most significant chapters in your own personal book is located within the physical body in your right ventricle. That is a portion of your heart that is closest to the center of your being as it tips toward it. It is also closest to the soul. That pump there receives the blessing from the spiritual mother, which is connected to your soul. The pump pushes the blood over to the left ventricle and then lets it go through the auricle to get out. So you're getting in the right ventricle (looking from your right side, it's on your right side) what I would term a spiritual kiss from the soul of you. A hug, a nudge, an embrace, a confidence thing to go forward more is coming from the soul. So when you feel your heart changing a little bit from the solar plexus, understand there is a communication going on from very ancient entities involved with your spiritual progress.

They are here to help now, and as that begins to take place, the grand chakra in your back (which is where your astrological chart is) begins to be vibrated and activated because of the spiritual forces of the planets that want to assist. They don't want to limit you; that has never been the case. They want to assist. The limitations are there so that you won't damage yourself, pretty much. The spiritual forces of those planets want to assist in your graduation, your preparation, and your performance. That's what it's for. Yet there are those who know this and have restricted information on the proper use. It's an electrical diagram for your self in the ability to use proper thought frequencies. It comes in at angles. You just have to know the train tracks and who's talking to you and when. This is the process you're going through now. It's the process. It's the process.

That significance of Christ on the cross was supposed to be understood. He did it — with all of his personalities — so you don't have to. That's why it was done: so that it doesn't have to be done again. Yet everybody wants the replication. Why? Because there is no understanding. He did the performance on the cross thing. Even with the words and the other understandings, you have another understanding here that has been spoken of, okay, but it's not *out there*. This understanding is that there was another one who took his place yet is still in the connection of it.

So you're working with beings. Well, you're not working with them; they're working against you. In the proper functioning of the truth and how things are performed, I will put it that way. Everyone has his or her jurisdiction: This church has this jurisdiction; that church has that jurisdiction. "They are the only ones that are right." "These are the only ones that are right," and they are confusing everyone and trying to control with the funds, the money, and the beings. You are realizing that now. You have this dignity that's been lost in the understanding of spiritual truths.

Identify Your Foundation

You're in the change now. In this September and October [2015] that you went through, you found out that a lot of the bricks in your foundation are cracked, are cracked. What *is* your foundation? Well, it depends on your posture. If you're sitting, your foundation is in your pelvis. If you're standing, your foundation is in your legs. It changes. What is your thought process at each level of foundation?

If you're laying on your back, your foundation is in the spine of your back. So you have to understand that you are a cubic function within the context of the magnetic and electrical forces.

Now, the cubic function is a function of the mind — the cubic function of the mind. That's behind you. That's behind you. You're coming out of the cubic function of the mind into free space, which is all space. It is all space. So you're going through the process of reversing engines. We have said before that you need to start backing up in yourself a little bit now. But now there is an engine reversal needed, and you're going to have to backpedal because you're seeing everyone else going over the falls. They'll go over, and they're not sure why or how, but they're going over because there is nothing to hold on to. They forgot themselves.

The Spirit Ophiel

This spirit Ophiel is going to begin to allow itself to be present. This is a Holy Spirit, one of the holy ones, and cleanliness is required, number one. The performance of his duties is the transformation of the physical body. I don't mean from life into death and then reincarnate. That is not what I mean. I mean the transformation of it literally, healing in a minute, fixing it. He does it, and he knows how to do it, just the acceptance of it.

Some people, once they have a little fix, they say, "All my pain went away. Where did it go?" And they look for it again and get it back. You found it. Now what are you going to do with it? So how do you educate that type of being? They should accept the healing and go forward. Don't go looking for the old stuff, or you will get it back again, and then you're going to complain again. This is exactly what is going on now. It is a repetition in the old mind. It is behind you. Go forward, actually. Just go forward up at an angle, about a 45-degree angle. It comes out of the solar plexus and goes up as a gold ladder. Your little self, your inner self, walks it.

The Ten Commandments — everybody has broken them. Don't worry about it; just don't do it again, that's all. Walk the ladder, up the ladder, up the ladder. Ask for forgiveness. You know what you did; no one has to tell you what you did. You *know* what you did. You absolutely know, and you knew it when you were a kid. When you were two years old throwing your tantrums, you knew exactly what you were doing. That knowledge is still there, so it's time for everyone to grow up. This is what is happening now, and there isn't going to be anyone to blame. You're going to be standing as a stalk in your own wind when this thing hits.

Then there will be those looking forward to help and will bring everyone together and see whether you're okay. You're going through this. What we have caused is a pause, which is going on this week (first week of September). Slow down so that everyone can reconstitute and coalesce what happened. Now, you go and proceed from that point. A lot of beings are cleaning, so you're going to proceed from that point up and then go back. You're going to start getting things in order and making it easier to keep clean: Move this here. Move this there. Then you only have to do a little bit, not a lot. That is what is going on in consciousness and within the system of the self called the holy part of you that knows this, you know?

Within the human condition, there are only really three holy portals. The trinity of yourself. It is the job of each individual ego to understand the trinity of the self to bring it together. It's the Father-Son-Holy Spirit, yet it's not a male-female thing. You are an electrical-magnetic understanding of self.

Electric, magnetic, and what's the third one?

Your brain is present. Brain is the third one. The brain is the only thing you have that is present, that is providing the ability for the electrical-magnetic forces to work within the system of your self. The brain is the access. You have two halves. Sew them together with lavender light. Then it's a unified brain that also allows you the unified theory.

Oh, I have to have a unified brain to access ...

You have to have a unified brain so that you don't argue with yourself. The synapses go back and forth. The kundalini comes up one side, and the other kundalini comes up the other side. Then you have to have your clear kundalini in the center, these little guys, which balances those two kundalinis.

Then you don't need all that if you have the brain ...

If the brain is present! You have an overlord in your crown chakra that sits and looks down at the Buddha one. I might as well say that now. It sits there with its gold and silver helmet looking down and, "What are you guys doing down there? Straighten up and straighten the chakras." That's what is going on now, because it is ruling over the brain within the brain. It is your consciousness appreciation of yourself that you can even think. That's what lets you enjoy reading and enjoy all that stuff. It is your perfumed flower, if you want to understand it. It has petals, and each petal communicates and talks and does all of these things. In fact, all the chakras look like petals, and they communicate, but the shutdown in the human condition is an understanding of confusion that is probably not accomplished anywhere else. Here, they limited it to here, but it's a movement out.

November [2015], now, you are going to have to have your boots on. You're going to feel as if there's going to be a belt that goes across your stomach, and you'll feel it. It will be like a waistband to keep you conformed to yourself now, because there will be a great desire for expansion, but you want to expand correctly. You want to expand within yourself, upward and then downward. Everybody's expecting an ascension thing. I told you this is a descension thing. You will be doing the descending thing.

When the high self descends in you and the overself (there's three beings), you will ascend up into it, but you'll still be within the descended process. You will still be physical. There is no sense in dying the body and not knowing what you're doing again. You've already done that. It is to accomplish the task of passing through walls and objects easily without damage to the body or damage to the wall or object — transitioning of self, transitioning of self.

You have the abilities to do that. Yet the constructs that you are involved with now limit that ability because you are using time as a horizontal force. Time is a direction. It is up. It is not horizontal. Your clock is making it horizontal. It's a circular spiral force, actually. It spirals upward and comes down. It is really gravity, the being called Gravity, that establishes time in the phases. It's all involved with $E = mc^2$ over there [referring to the painting on the cover of *Totality and Beyond: The Search for the Origin of Life — and Beyond*, 2015, Light Technology Publishing]. That's the technique; that's how you do it. You understand that the speed of light spreads all energy, beings getting the mass and moving that fast.

You do that by saying, "I arise the vibration that I Am." You can only do it with your I Am-ness. You cannot do it with anything else. It takes seven keys to do that, one for each chakra. So if you meditate on your chakras in a point in time, "I arise the vibration that I Am" and bring it up to the next chakra. "I arise the vibration that I Am" and bring it up to the next chakra. Then, when you get all seven chakras, you bring it back into the grand chakra in your back, and you say, "I arise the vibration that I Am."

You have to call your spiritual guardians here — Michael, Raphael, Gabriel, Uriel — and put them in there. They know where they are. You'll be in the center of that, and they will assist in balancing the space for you so that you can succeed in doing it. This is the job of the humans to do it. This is where you do it. You become here. You become more. You become more. You become more. You learn. You are going to learn eventually. That is what eternity is about. The movement of the magnetic construct to the electrical construct is a movement of density into freedom.

Magnets are dense, electricity moves, and the space in between is the freedom part. That is where your human condition is, between the magnetic and pure electricity. You are in between there, and you are resonating between both. You just need to know how to understand them as a force, and the importance of water within this force, because water allows the movement of the thoughts so that manifestation can occur between the electrical and the magnetic, which is your body.

The significance of yourself has been misunderstood because you came from one seed and all the organs and everything developed out of that. Isn't that a miracle? Does anybody really understand how that happened? You had no idea how it became. Yet you're going through it now because you're going through the reverse end of the process. You are living your death because you've had a life, but your life was before the birth. So you are figuring yourself out in the process. You are, in a manner, living within your test tube of the self with dignified spiritual forces. And you are becoming something, whether you like it or not.

The dwelling part of it — and by dwelling I mean when you focus on your negativities that everyone else is doing to you, the "oh, the poor victim" thing, "What have you done!" — is that you, focus on clearing yourself for a new presence. You have a brain that is always present. It is not behind you. It is with you. The mind is behind you. If you go to another country and haven't studied the culture, you're not going to know anything, but you will have a brain with you that can help you work your way through it. Your old world consciousness isn't going to help anything — maybe learn how to start a fire, that memory thing.

You are moving into a new presence now; literally you are. By the time you read this, you're going to be in a new presence. Now, what are you going to do with this new presence? Remember what it took to get you here, in a manner, but don't reflect on having to go through that again. Take the opportunity to understand the beautiful presence of your brain now, and acknowledge the brain. There is a being, actually two beings, there. There are guardians there, and when you start working with them, you're going to find a lot of humor, a lot of joy, and a lot of unexpected pleasures. I will put it that way. The bones will really begin to sing. Your fingers will sing.

CHAPTER

10

The Power of the Grand Chakra

September 8, 2015

Now, as the movement of the heart speaking … it's not channeling. It is the interior expression expounding. It's like a little one, a baby, learning its first words. It speaks the words, sees the reaction, speaks the words, watches the reaction. Babies know, mentally, that they are in the process of conforming to the system they are in. They figure things out. They already know, and they are watching the results of others' actions and learning in the meantime how to participate within that and still maintain a self. Now, that is the heart of the baby thinking, the brain of the baby analyzing, and the mind of the baby figuring it out.

You are going through that same process now. The heart wants to speak, and when the heart speaks, it wants to speak what it knows, its truth. It knows all of the lies. It knows all of it. As it matures — by mature, I mean the membrane. We'll call it a membrane. It's not really a membrane; it's a field. It's an electromagnetic field that is accessed by other entities you are not aware of, and the access is gained by watching news media and listening to everyone else's words, because you interpret it.

The movement there for the heart, now, it's going to refuse to entertain those other ideas and thoughts. It wants to express itself clearly as a unit. The confusion comes when sometimes it is a necessity to fit in. While the heart doesn't want to fit in, it wants now to know itself. It will speak and defend itself now, and by that, I mean the speech from the heart can stop anything in its tracks — any moving creature, animals and humans included. When a heart speaks, other hearts know it immediately, and they have a desire themselves to be able to speak in response to that one speaking in an appropriate manner. But the brain does not understand that yet. The mind has not had that experience yet. So the confusion comes, and anger starts welling up in others who haven't allowed their hearts to speak. They could drop dead, literally, or fall down or faint, because when a heart talks to a heart there will be an answer from the heart. It might not resonate with the physical form that the one heart is in, and it could drop. It will stop it. The brain has to, now, reestablish a connection with the heart, for the heart speaks. The synapses in the brain, both the left side and the right side, and the unification of the brain with the lavender flame going back and forth — so you have one unified brain where the synapses function appropriately in response to the pleasure and need of the heart.

So there is a link that has to become established, and it's going to need to pass through the throat chakra, down to the solar plexus, and up to the heart. That is the channel the path follows, down and up and skip to throat. The expression coming out of the chest, it will be like you have a speaker membrane here, like you plug your speakers into your music devices. That membrane is your chest. That's there. That's there, and it's just on the opposite side of your astrological chart. So you'll be talking or speaking with the force of the planetary systems that you have inscribed on your back. That is what the heart knows. We have told you this before.

The consciousness unit that has been established as a heart in you is your next incarnation. The heart, not your mind, carries the memories, and they are in the four chambers. There are four chambers there, well, actually five. There's one in the middle, that little cave that you're not aware of yet. Each chamber has a beat (the heart beat), and each beat is a thought. Along with the thought, there is an expression there. But in the beat is a sound, and with the sound, there is color. With color, there is formation and manifestation. You are going to learn how to do that with the beat of your heart and walk to your own tones, which are in your bones.

You have a unique system — by "you," I mean the planetary human condition — locked and blessed that you can produce yourself knowingly. You are going through this suppression routine now coming out from the influence, we are going to say, of evil. You're becoming aware of it, and the heart is beating with your conscious attainment of a greater self than evil can handle.

You are going to rise above this distortion, and as you do, then the others see and do. Now, in the first steps of the process, the only time beings seemed to pay attention to themselves, in a manner, for discipline and dignity, the only way they get back to that point within themselves is when they go through an illness or damage the body. Then they have to reflect and slow down — "What has happened here?" — because you are fighting the demon that wants to kill you, or die you, I will say, not kill you. They can't kill you. They die you. They just put you some place you agree to until you figure out you don't need to be there. This is the frequency you are going through now. This is the frequency.

All Hearts Are Equal

One of the most difficult things to get through in this time and space is the understanding of the nature of religion and the understanding of consciousness. Your United States has a consciousness and a language of the American people, basically. The United States has a consciousness, Germany has a consciousness, Mexico has a consciousness, and Brazil has a consciousness — units, they think and act differently. You use different words, different expressions, and different emotional force in speech, all of these things, for manipulation of consciousness.

Now, you can take that back to this Tower of Babel thing. You're coming out of that. The heart knows it because the heart speaks to all in creation that have hearts. That is consciousness. It is a consciousness unit that is the same for every heart on the planet, the knowing it has nothing to do with countries, but your speech and your attitudes and your customs do. The heart has four beats and thinks when it's going to speak. When this begins to occur in everyone, it is going to shift ones in the ability to stay alive. You are already seeing the distortion in your world today with equality. There is no equality, yet all hearts are equal. The consciousness units involved have been overlaid by a surreptitious force that has no desire for the completion and understanding of, what you term, the soul. The human condition does not know what a soul is. It knows possibly what the idea of the soul is because there are words used to describe it. It has no idea of the feeling yet, unless you get into the heart talk.

The heart desires to perform its duty for the body. The soul desires to get out of the body to perform a greater duty. Right now, those two are working together, and the souls now are choosing to stay in the body and understand the wisdom of the heart. How did the heart become the heart? For that matter, how did your liver become the liver and your lungs become the lungs out of one seed? Who did that? You did know how to do it. You were a parasite on your mother's system for bones. So the heart knows how it did it, and that is the wisdom of the self coming up. As you say, the heart suffers a lot because it knows.

The heart desires to be embraced, yet it can't be. It has to feel the embrace through all the other layers. It is necessary to feel the embrace through all the other layers because it is such a delicate instrument that it could be damaged with the thought. So the brain needs to understand the thought process required in the communication with the heart. In other words, the heart is going to speak, so the brain shuts up. By "brain shuts up," I mean do not access the mind that is past and behind you. Access your present space, pay attention to the beat of your body, and listen to the resonance within your bones.

This is the opportunity within the human condition to manifest in the hand. This is the opportunity where the human condition can allow itself to be healed in a moment. This is the opportunity for the human condition to understand itself as a human one, as a spiritual one, as a being who exists forever in the understanding of everywhere and everywhen. So you are collecting your pieces, eventually. You're in that process now.

This is where the mind can be of an advantage, the new superior one mind, that you know the mind has an understanding that is greater than this one unit, yet this one unit is going to incorporate all its other units. It has the opportunity to know when you get through arguing with the selves in here, in the body. The healing modality coming is available for everyone on the planet. The only way you're going to succeed with it is to quiet the mind and allow the heart to move in the correct manner because it is a movement in the genetic requirement.

Beings like to use the DNA thing, where the heart has a sense to move toward the middle. Initially you are going to get that sense when you have, basically, a desire to surrender, to know more, to receive more, and then be able to receive it and work with it with a different organ dominating the thought process. Right now if you asked any human — anyone — which organ in the body dominates the thought process, depending on the generational gaps, you will find the root chakra predominant, naval chakra maybe, that hunger thing.

Listen to the Heart Speak

The human condition is going to learn who is ruling it. You are ruling yourself for dominance. Why and how is the influence of you not you? You have leaders who are not leaders. You have corruption in high places. As the cleansing begins, you're seeing the arrogance become more profound and more disdainful due to the condition of others. You are in that process right now.

Now, this place of healing that is going to be established, beings are setting it up. It's the first step in introducing you to the knowledge of your self. The three rings are simply three rings, circles, nothing magical about them, except that they hold frequency at different levels within each ring. As you walk through the rings, you feel it. You change. In the center ring, you have this experience of what is ascension, basically. When you get to the third ring, you will literally be able to lift your body in the air without doing anything. You will understand the transformation process from dying to living. As you come through your back, you will feel the force of the death that you've been working on, because that's what you're working on, literally, your death.

When you understand this, then the health becomes easier for you, no matter where you are. The knowledge and support of energy of death, you will find, stimulates you to a greater understanding of not being dead because you have overcome this concept of what life is not. So the healing process is more, really, the process of acknowledging the divinity of self and the forever of self. This potential that you will be able to realize is that you can disappear your body at this moment and appear it over here and then reappear.

Now, you have been told that your Sedona area is a place where you beings could just walk, lay the body down, and come back into the body, no matter where you were in that area, no matter where. Nobody would disturb it. Well, that's not the condition now, obviously. You're into that moving from sacred to holy. That's a very serious step. Then you have to go to another level of holy, which is more serious.

Then you are going to have to understand your sex. Why are you female? Why are you male? And don't go into the fault of it because you did it. There is an acceptance and a request there. You have to understand that it was yours. You have to get that part down, and you will find out why when you listen to the heart speak, not to what someone else says. It is going to start off with the heart speaking as a drumbeat, and your mediums now are going through that process. Some of it is shocking them because they weren't expecting this. It is not a channeling/mediumship thing. It is a graduation thing, an acknowledgment that you have gotten this far. Then your demeanor is different because you have a superior being now that you have recognized that is inside you, and you don't need another one to contact with it because all hearts talk the same language. You are in that phase. There will not be many who go through in this arena, because they won't accept the heart speaking. It's too much truth.

Now, you have heard the term 144,000. Those are consciousness units in each individual body. You have 144,000; someone else has 144,000. They are all there, and they are the ones that the identity/ego/self said they were educated or would be there for the enlightenment within the self. So those 144,000 units — some beings will call them cells, but they are units of consciousness — as they gather to encourage and strengthen the heart in its ability to speak, they are the ones who move into holy. That has been written about.

The144,000 are inside you. You just need to put them in the proper position, and the proper position is an alignment in the center of your being. Center yourself. The seven chakras align them. The forty-nine personalities align them. The forty-ninth knows the seven. There is a different seal for each chakra. Those seals were given as authority for the chakra. It's like a diploma, if you wish, but that is very simplistic, because there is power there. Within that power, there is the ability to do things and make things happen without going anywhere, simply by the thought of it and knowing where within the being/body the thought is coming from for the action to be performed outside of itself by others. So it has a control function here. You are a pilot or driving your car. You're the one doing all of it. You have to pay attention to reflexes, visuals, and all of this as you're driving. So too you have to pay attention to the changes occurring within you.

How? This is the tricky part, how your force of perception influences the condition of the physical from within. What you are finding out as you move further through this is that at each moment, you are standing in your death and presenting yourself, but you're moving through it. "Health to the body, mind, and spirit" is a phrase that should be utilized for yourself because it is confirmation to your self. Health to the body, health to the mind — that is, healing the mind for past indulgences. Health to the spirit, because you in the human condition have been corrupting your spirit, your spirit, your spirit. The Holy Spirit is the one that is introducing you to this process by allowing you to have blood so that you can perform your duties and have a heart to learn from.

Nature Knows

Nature is changing. She is responding heart to heart. That is why you are seeing and witnessing animals working with other animals, different species and things. They know what is coming, what's coming. They know how to balance it. They are trying to balance it. The expression of the Buddha was one of compassion for those who suffered, working to assist the suffering and not simply indulging himself in the wealth that he had. Yet you have beings in your world now, and all they think of is wealth. They have done nothing for others, and they will never do anything for others. When the screaming starts about how they are going to need assistance, no one is going to help them.

This process is not evident, yet you have armies all over the world moving into positions to control, what is termed, a societal condition. It used to be you had a church "here," a religion "here," a religion "here," and a religion "here." Each religion controlled or attempted to control the consciousness of those involved in that religion instead of teaching. There is control "here," control "there," threat, threat, threat, threat. You have succeeded in creating threats everywhere. You're going to live through them, but you might not like the process of going through it or the unbelievable criminality about to be purported over the human condition.

You are about to go through an experience of criminality of

consciousness trying to control the human condition. You're going to realize it now. It's no longer a theory. You will not be able to converse with certain ones without creating conflict. They don't want to hear it anymore. There is a vengeance coming, and it's not from, what you call, the holy ones, either.

So you have an issue here where the hearts know and haven't done anything. The brain is trying to reestablish itself in, what you call, its physical condition. That is why the requirement for healing: people know inside themselves there needs to be healing. They just don't know what it is. They'll be allowed this great expansion. As it happens, there is a "craziness" that develops. I have to use that word, for as you go through this thing, you'll think you're finally through. Then you're going to go into the same things you did before and try again. It's not going to work.

Your new personalities are coming up with new skills and (how you say?) new procedures and abilities of profound nature for the benefit of all. You are going to need to think in union with the beat of your heart from auricle to ventricle to ventricle to auricle from auricle to ventricle to ventricle to auricle throughout the system. You're going to realize the importance of each beat of self. As the heart chakra opens, the cognizant knowledge that comes from the right auricle receiving the blood back into the body for oxygenation opens the heart chakra. As it goes down through the ventricle to the pump, the right ventricle, it has a feeling of comfort and relaxation. As it goes through the left ventricle, it prepares itself with all of the thoughts that you had while it was in the left ventricle. It prepares itself to push it to the left auricle to be pumped out of the body. So your preparation of your thought form is in your left ventricle. As it gets to the left auricle, that thought form, those desires, those innuendos — all of it that you are contemplating in the left and right ventricles — are going off to the body for manifestation.

In the meantime, more blood is coming back in. But you don't think of that, how you manifest. You don't follow the beat of your heart. You are looking for your mind, and that is behind you. You've already done that. You've done it! What did you learn? Nothing. You have learned you have to keep going. There is more. There's more with the beat of the heart. The other thing that you are not aware of, though, in the metaphysical understanding, is Earth is taking a lot of the punishment. Earth is also a drum. It has a beat to it, a drumbeat, a beat, as each planet does. As those beats begin to synchronize the realization within the self, you will feel them in the grand chakra in your back, the beat of the planets and the beat of Earth in conjunction with those.

You will begin to walk along with those beats because you know the perpetuosity of yourself, and you are a forever being. You remove the fear because the heart is working, and with proper thought, the heart will always work. It is improper thought that stops the heart. You have sent it out yourself with all your words, because the left ventricle takes a lot of worrying and concerns there. It does. All the fear and things just accumulate there. Yet you must pleasure yourself, and this is where peace, protection, and joy are needed there, particularly in that ventricle. Health to the body, mind, and spirit when it gets to the right and left auricles so that you can push out.

You should thank the Holy Spirit for that blood, because if it didn't squeeze your bones, you wouldn't have any. That's how it works. So thankfulness first, always, in the water you drink, the food you eat, and the air you breathe. You will understand air differently in the next couple of weeks.

The right auricle needs to be thanked. The right auricle needs to thank the Holy Spirit for producing the blood. Then you will begin to know yourself in connection with different things. [Loud burst of thunder.] That was a little adjustment. The right auricle is the Holy Spirit in the bones; then you are going to find out that that is you. You're going to find out something else. You are going to find out that that is the force of Jesus in you. That's what you're going to find out. That was the mystery of Christ, one of them.

Consciousness Changes

There are many beings. There are powers and principalities. You've heard of those phrases, and there are forgivers of sins. They have called, and there are powers there for the healing of it, because the greatest enemy in the human condition is the spiritual shame you are going to have for not cleaning your self up, regardless of what another does. It's the shame that limits your ability. It's a shame thing because what it is, the shame, is you disregarded your knowing — what you knew! You thought you could get away with something, and you didn't.

There are laws, spiritual laws. When anybody makes up his or her own, that's another thing, but there are profound spiritual laws. All people know what they are, and you argued around them. Then you found yourself in a quagmire because you didn't obey them, and you joined the side that argued against them. That's the shame of it, when you find out what holy is. The heart knows this, and the hearts are going to speak and are going to refuse to be controlled now in a way that is not beneficial to the system itself.

Diets are going to change. You're already aware of this GMO stuff, but there's another form of food being made available in the astral, in a manner. It's spiritual food. It's proper thought. When you have proper thought and you have need for another sustenance, it is going to change because you will find out that you manifested the food inside the self. You don't need to grab and put. So you are in that knowing of self and the requirement of it.

It is like this thing with Jesus and the wine. We have to use these stories because you have heard them and know about them, but it's also the performance of you. When he was serving the wine at the wedding feast and there was not enough — his mother said there was not enough — he said to have faith, and there was always enough because consciousness changes. You are going to learn that within the self because Jesus's energy, his energy, we're going to use that phrase, is in there between your heart and your bones, teaching you to be thankful for the Holy Spirit that produces your blood.

Now, if beings would understand this and move about their world producing something for themselves and others, then you wouldn't have all this conflict. But you have beings who do not want to do that. They think they are more worthy. Everyone is the same, pretty much. You're going to find out that you are all equal and pretty much all look alike. But you don't understand that yet. You are going to understand this. It's called the wall of shame. This is where many beings are going to stand in front of it, and they're going to see it.

You can't go anywhere because it is your shame. It is shown. Then you have a reflection on it, and in that reflection, you move into a deeper level of shame. In that reflection, you are stuck in the quagmire until another one has this authority over you in a way to forgive the sins. Those beings have been called. Those forgivers of sins are in the Pistis Sophia, which are the entities Faith and Wisdom who fell, as you understand it, and whom Jesus came to readjust. They fell because of doubt. That's all it was, pretty much. We'll call it the fall.

You have an understanding of the fall. Pretty much, all people have had dreams in which they fall back into the body. You fell into something from somewhere and you're here. So that is a reminder of a greater fall that had taken place. You don't have to go into whatever; you're coming out of that now. This is the time when you're going to need ones — those who understand the difference between sacred and holy. Those are the ones who are going to hold the stability. They are not going to judge anything, no. They are just going to sit there broadcasting light, peace, and faith for those beings who want it. It's a whole other thing in the authority of the self and the knowledge of where and when it is.

There is authority there. The heart will speak with that authority, and things get done. Things are performed, we'll put it that way. Everyone here is performing some function, and they don't know what it is. You're performing a service with the divine influence that has a desire to perpetuate the human condition. There are not many beings who want to perpetuate the human condition. There are those who just want to overlord it and think they are it. That is what is changing now. That is what is changing.

You think you can get away from spiritual doctrine, but you can't because it is in your hands — in your thumbs and your fingers, both hands. It's in your toes. Prayers are written on the bones in your legs and in your feet. When you walk, you're praying, but you don't know it. Those are ancient prayers you were thinking (when you were in the fetus) for protection of the self.

Now, if you allowed yourselves to reflect on the beauty of your mother when you were in the fetus, you would know what those prayers are. Yet there's much antagonism and things toward the mother and the spiritual mother. What beings don't realize is your mother had it harder than you did, and her mother had it harder than she did. Her mother had it harder than she did. The whole lineage is a struggle, and now it's time to understand that and pull everyone up because you are the worth that they prayed for. You are the worth that they prayed for to get them out of their struggle. You are the answer to those prayers, whether you know it or not. You volunteered for it, whether you know it or not. That is why you are here, and that's why you were born, number one, as an aid to the parental system. You answered prayers even for those of little faith to bring the faith, because you understand this faith, knowledge of the presence, whatever it is. That is growing up. You are continually in this process of growing up, yet there are ones who don't want to. They don't want to. They don't want to.

Saving lives is the nature of humanity, pretty much — or was initially for community. Then there came an alteration, and you are going through that alteration now, collectively in humanity all over your planet. These are the last throws of the dice for those ones. As the ones of the heart begin to speak, they will gather together. There will be a gathering in a place after what happens happens. It will just be a natural thing. There will be those who want to intrude there, but they won't succeed in spatial terms. As you say, you protect the space within the meditation so that you can have safety there under proper influence.

The Grand Chakra

What most people do not realize is as you move from area to area — say, from Sedona you just drive coming to Flagstaff or another region — the human condition doesn't ask permission to enter spiritual regions. You should ask permission to enter because there are spiritual guides there. But humans just drive, drive, drive. You go anywhere. No. You should ask permission to enter a particular space. It has to be granted, and you accept it. You behave differently in that space. You have to because you knew you had to ask permission so that the different spiritual laws are abided by there. But that knowledge is not perpetuated. Beings think they can just go anywhere anytime they want without regard to the spiritual forces that are there protecting the human condition that is there — or working with them, anyway. So you are facing things now.

You're noticing your weather's changing. You are noticing, or some have, your earthquakes are increasing. Your volcanoes are increasing. You have die-offs in your whales from the Fukushima thing — sea lions and birds too. The radiation off the California coastline is going off the chart. It is in the air, and it's affecting the soil. You're going to get a reaction from the mother. The planet is going to adjust her skirt.

The protection of space, spiritually speaking, has not been taught yet. You have learned the fundamentals. You have learned the basics — candles and incense and prayers. That's what you've learned so far. That is all you've learned, and you hope it works, because you're really not sure whether it does. It smells nice when you light the incense. It changes some things. Spirits can dance around the flames. But that's not performing the spiritual protection you are going to need to develop. It is going to be required, and this will be given by Shiva, actually, certain prayers or mantras just for the protection of space. Om Mani Padme Hum is one. It protects the space because the spirits of the space know what that means — who gave it, who runs it, and who owns it. That's why you use it. Even if you don't know, they know. They know.

When it [Om Mani Padme Hum] is running, the vibratory frequency imbues your body so that your cellular structure attunes to it, and you begin to know. You begin to feel it. You begin to access the power that exists in that grand chakra in your back. Now, no one has talked about the grand chakra except us, and no one knows how to use it except us. You are learning it. It's the presence where the Holy Spirit can talk through you. It activates the systems in there, those little clauses you signed when you passed Jupiter and Mars and passed Venus and Mercury and Pluto and Neptune. They are there, and they remember you. You are going to remember them in the essence and the purpose of them. That is what that grand chakra is for. You are the physical expression of those forces casting forward.

The old phrase is "back up." Back up into yourself. Then you will see the Sun that is here in the heart chakra. You will see and feel the eyes above the Sun in the heart chakra, and you're not so interested in what you like, but you're interested in the self that is there for assistance for ones who need to know there is more. It is not just live a life, suffer, and die. That is not the purpose of this place, but that's what's going on, and that's going to change for those who have the understanding of God — the knowledge of a moreness that created you and how you created yourself, all of it, the equality there and then the worthiness.

"The worthiness" is another phrase that needs to be understood. The ants are worthy. The bees are worthy, butterflies. There are not many in the human condition, if you compare them to the ants and the bees, that can say they are as worthy. The ants and the bees know what they're doing; they are perpetuating the hive in the colony. But does the human condition do the same equally here, as such? No, it doesn't. But the human condition here, consciousness countries, people together — put your ant colony "here." Put your beehive "here," and see who's working and worthy for what the life force is. It's for others, not just the self. It is for others. So they can have an idea that they can be something — anything — eventually be what they want to be. That is the process. That was the teaching of Jesus, the teaching of Buddha, and the teaching of Gandhi — same thing, same thing. So having it been that way and anyone understand it, look at what you have. You have more weapons now to destroy and blow this Earth up ten times over. Well, you won't. We are going to see what we can do to slow that process down.

The movement now is toward a greater understanding of the equality of everyone. Everyone is equal. The hearts beat the same, except for some that have arrhythmia and all that little nonsense, because that is their thought not thinking right. The brain hasn't been trained right. It is responding in anger. The mind, that is what you know. It hasn't been trained right. That has to be allowed to change, and that is why beings grow up, so that you can learn something and proceed. You're still growing up. You haven't grown up yet! Some think they are going to grow up if they die or commit suicide, which seems very popular now, but it doesn't work that way.

The Energy of Love Is an Invisible Wave

Walking around in ignorance, you are as dead as you will ever be. Committing suicide, you're going to go back three steps and reclaim everything you thought was bad for you. You have to. That is what is going on now. You have people in your local area just jumping off bridges. There was no assistance available. They did know where to look or didn't want to. The argument of self being more dramatic than the space, that's not intelligent at all. It's what happens when this suicide thing happens. It is basically that you thought you could rule someone, and you found out you couldn't. Nobody wants your worth now, whatever you think you're worth is, because you haven't proven it. Then that sense of shame comes, and then there is just doubt.

It is not the being who committed suicide who did it. It's the one who influences that being with the voice to do it. No one trained him or her about that voice. You are in that now, so you have to be careful what you listen to and how you listen. Center your being in the chakras, seven. Then go to the forty-ninth and receive, and listen to your heart. It is that simple. It is that simple.

When you pull in the dynamics of yourself through tradition, your light becomes so bright that beings cannot even look at you, so you have to tone it down. Then you have to understand you have much more light and wisdom than required. Then you become that. The energy of love is a wave of lavender and gold and green. All it likes to do is love; it just wants to love, embrace, love, and move through. It doesn't sit. It loves. It heals and looks back at times to see how it moves, and then it moves to another one. It comes over the mountains as a wave. You can't see it. It's an invisible wave. It moves through everything and sees everything.

There's another force there that looks for anything that is alive to kill, because it has a jealousy factor. It doesn't know itself yet, the equality there. This is the energy the human planet is going through now. That's why there's so much war. It's ignorance in its supreme form, and no one can argue that one. It's displayed.

So blessings peace, protection, and joy. Remember the heart speaks, and the brain speaks. Remember particularly the diaphragm, as you move it, as the heart beats. Remember the four chambers. Remember the secret chamber in the middle because that is where your light spark is. White brilliant light, tiny but powerful, and it is the one educating you and itself in the process of the brilliance of yourself, the divine force.

In this healing center, there won't be a big crowd to come, one or two at a time. They will just go through. They'll know who is at each level and who they're speaking with, and no one will have to say anything. Then the appreciation will be there and the recognition, and then they go. Then eventually the word spreads, and people will come. Then we will have to set some boundaries. That's not established yet, but that's the process. One of the difficulties we will have is those who have healed through this have a tendency to be egocentric, and then they lose the humility of the system and damage themselves. So we have to be very careful with this thing, these forces.

They are invisible yet know how to make themselves visible. They don't speak; they *do*. They do not speak. They do not lecture. They perform, like the ants and the bees. You are going to meet them in the performance of your duties.

Okay, thank you, thank you.

You're welcome. We are through.

CHAPTER

11

God's Path Is through the Water

September 15, 2015

Part of the process that the human condition is in is the process of waking up within the physical body. You are in the condition now of walking around with an ego that owns the body, its movements and things. Yet that's the exterior manipulative consciousness that you've been trained with. That's how you develop an ego, the newer self, when you came out of the womb. You had the experience. You knew it. That's knowing. Fitting in with consciousness as you are growing up, you are trying to adjust to others knowing.

You access certain conditions to feel comfortable in the presence of other beings. You adjust and adapt. Your feelings make that change for you: "I like 'that.' I don't like 'that.'" That thing. The humans have grown up with that adjustment facility condition within them, and along with that comes the tablets of judgment that you carry: You don't like "this." You like "that." You have the inability as a little one to change your environment. No one has taught you, and your elders did not know how to do it, either. Memories of the things, of those specific abilities, that can alter environments and change circumstances are caught and trapped in the different religions you have. The force, the being — it's not a being, and it wasn't a being when it started this thing, the whole thing, all of the pieces. You had your prophets and your messiahs and your leaders and you teachers through the centuries receiving specific information for "this" and "that." Each one was better than the other, and there was always a correction coming from somewhere that made sense. Even though it was coming from different religions, you responded to it. You understood part of it.

Now beings are anticipating the Christ, the antichrist, anticipating a lot of things. How would you know? How would you know? You wouldn't know. You can't tell the difference between the antichrist and the Christ. You think you'll be able to, but you haven't trained yourself in the understanding of how and why you were born. How did that happen? That's because your mother and father, your parents, had sex, and you came out of that union. How did you get there? You didn't just first start there. So the conscious connection now is starting to be made — the hows and the whys — because you said you would. That's why, and number two, because you were sent; that's why. By whom? That's up to you to figure out. You're going to figure it out because you have heard of the term "reincarnation." You might not remember your incarnation past, and you might not remember the time frame sequence. You're going through this expansion now.

What is going to stun everybody is when the space begins to talk to you. You're going to think it's a being. There are beings who are going to do that. They are trying to influence your mental capacity. They are trying to see which antennae within you they can activate to get your attention. Yet discernment hasn't been developed to notice the inflections within the voice, whether it is for your benefit or the benefit of the entity influencing you.

You haven't learned to understand voices yet that are from the outside or the inside. You haven't categorized from what direction they are coming because you don't know. You have these ones in mental hospitals who have these, you call them, hallucinations and experiences with other entities and all these things. Well, it's going to become more apparent that that is what is the normal communication pattern now.

The consciousness stream in your human condition is trying to influence you by your news media, your readings, and your visual reception of data from movies. That's an influence on you. Your decision-making process of choosing proper influences on you, for you, that discernment ability has not been trained within you. Who's the falsifier, and who's not? "This" is healthy for you, and "this" is not. You have symptoms you develop in your body when illness takes hold. You have pain in your body when an inappropriate behavior takes hold.

You're going through this adjustment process now with communicating with extraterrestrials and other entities in space, spatial differentials, for containment of the precious element of safety. You need safety if you're going to learn and function appropriately in the position and category you are in. You need the safety to learn that. This is what's trying to be established now, the safety part where the mind has no concept yet. The mind is behind you. You know what you've done and how you've accomplished it. You know what safe is from the past and what isn't. Yet you are developing a conscious entity within you that utilizes your brain and the heart at the same time in conjunction with understanding the needs of the soul, which is the primary beingness of you, the Buddha one of your self, I call it. There are other names, but this is what you're going through now.

Humans Need to Develop Communication with the Elemental Kingdom

When you are born, you have your mother and father there — well, at least your mother — when you come out of the womb. When you die, unless you know what you are doing, you have nobody there. You're in a conundrum. But you always have your guides and spiritual forces there. The acknowledgment of those spiritual forces needs to be imbued now in the physical condition. So you pick up a new family connection. This is what is beginning to happen. Your spiritual family, the beings in your world call them tribes, are coming together.

Many nationalities are in your tribe. Many comrades are there for you, and the opening to that memory of it will allow the confidence of your inner structure to take hold. You will be in the movement of what is going to be termed "heart speak," because the heart doesn't really want to chat a lot. It is familiar with four beats and is working on the fifth beat, which is that light in the cave at the junction of the auricles and ventricles. That is the fifth beat, and that is the fifth beat that works with the soul and communicates with the soul. It is a divine white brilliant light. It is beyond brilliant. You can't even look at it, really. You will be fried. That is what communicates with the soul part of you that sits in your solar plexus in the Buddha position as a golden entity.

The form of that being wants to expand within you. In other words, come out of the lotus position and extend the feet and legs through the appropriate feet and legs of you, and raise its head up into your head. Its whole body will extend from within you. It is the golden force of your self. We will term it the divine knowledge force. That particular entity of self is aware of being in a meditation from a higher Buddha one. It is aware of it.

As the connection begins to become established, you are in a meditation now, but you don't realize it — from the meditator of the meditating one out there and the meditating one, you. The meditator is the golden lightbeing of your self. You expand it, and it meets in between. You are going through that process now. That's why all these wars and all these damaging forces that are seeking to take control of the human consciousness are having a hard time and expending their last breaths, so to speak, in this war thing. They want their dominion from what they decide they think is their dominion.

But what's going to happen is you're going to see who's the one meditating through you and who you are reacting with under the meditator. You are in a meditation; you just have not connected to the one meditating you. He's allowing the experience that hasn't totally been accumulated in the wisdom of self there to be experienced by you in the wisdom of your self through the feelings, because the soul is a feeling entity. Now, it is a pyramidal form, as you develop, start, so you have a lot of latitude at the bottom. You can move back and forth and complain, yell, and scream, or don't do anything. But as you get up to the top, there is only one place to go, and that is up to the apex, which is the crown chakra — which when you do it, it opens the solar plexus.

That organ, when it opens, it opens. It's a chakra; it will open like a flower, and light will come out of it. Then the other chakras start opening and responding, and the crown chakra has to take charge. But you have to know who is there taking charge within the crown. This is the process you're going through. Everybody is going through the process of identifying themselves, and they're afraid of it. You might find out who you really are, and it isn't who you really thought you were. When this thing moves, and you're in the process of it now, that is what is happening globally. That is why your weather is changing pretty dramatically, actually. It just hasn't quite hit the news yet. You only get the news when they think it's over. This is a continual movement going on.

The most difficult thing to understand is the water is moving on the surface of the planet. It's not simply coming down in rain. It's moving all over. It is causing difficulties because water has consciousness and is 70 percent of your self. So all water communicates with all water everywhere, all of the time. It knows what it is doing.

There is an entity that rules the water. Actually, in your spiritual traditions, there is a phrase, "God's path is through the water," through it. The path is through the water. That's how he walks through you and blesses you and gives you an understanding of your self. But that force does not take charge of the body. It can very easily, but it doesn't do that. It wants the system in the body to understand itself. It takes charge of the space. It alters space so that bodies will react to it because it knows that something shifted, and there's an adjustment that starts taking place — or a balance. That property of the movement of space within the condition called time is occurring now. It's occurring.

We have told you before, time is a direction. You have horizontal time when you are working with your clock, but you do not understand time as a perception of your self from a different arena. You have the horoscope engraved on your back. We have told you that. That is about to flip. Now it is vertical. It is about to flip horizontally energy-wise. You will be in the middle of that horoscope. You will be standing there in the middle of it. The planets, you will see the houses and the planets, and you'll feel the strings. Actually, there are a lot of strings, spiritual strings there, and you'll feel them. Then you'll understand what time is, what time is, and how the magic of time is introduced by the entity called water.

When you understand the water, you'll understand time. Then you have the entities with fire, air, and earth, those entities. They are rulers there. You have a king of fire, you have a king of water, you have a king of earth, and you have a king of air. Each one is responsible for that kingdom. Yet the human condition does not understand the elemental condition. You think you're better than. There's no communication with and appreciation for them. Kings are kings. Queens are queens. Princes are princes. In your physical world, that representation has been abused, not so in the elemental kingdoms.

You're going to find out that there are other lords and lordesses around you who haven't been acknowledged. They are going to introduce themselves in a manner that, well, for some it will be very comfortable but for others, the majority, very uncomfortable. It will cause confusion in the ability to think correctly. You don't know how to respond. This is where everyone starts talking at once. It will be like you're in a big auditorium, and everybody is saying something and nobody can understand anything because the inner essence of quietness hasn't been trained — composure in the circumstances, we're going to call it this, you're in the process (we're going to call them "circumstances" because that is what has been developed) of —in the overthrow of consciousness. That's what you're in.

Units of Consciousness

The United States of America has a certain consciousness. England has a certain consciousness. You call them customs. France has a certain consciousness. Germany, Russia, Syria, Egypt, Saudi Arabia,

Thailand, Vietnam, South America — each country is a different unit of consciousness. When you try to bring them all together, there's an argument, and that's what's going on. The military is eventually going to be used for its true purpose, the rescue of the innocents and not the killing of the innocents, but that hasn't developed yet.

You're in the process now where the condition on planet Earth, after this process you're in, will never be the same. You won't look fondly back on what you did to it. You will choose to forget it because you're going to have other abilities. We are going to call them powers because that's what you understand as the force that manipulates things. But you are going to get other powers that are beneficial for the self. One of the powers is the release of the fear and the doubt of the importance of the self. That's going to go away. The significance of the you of you is going to be what is the end result without the braggadocio thing the humans get into, the movie stars and things. It won't be like that.

You are going through the process of shamanic introduction, initiation if you will, as you'll be able to speak and communicate with animals. You will find that all communication is the same. It really is, basically. They have a recording of crickets, and one gentleman slowed the recording way down so that he could listen to it differently. Crickets life spans are really short, and when he slowed the recording down, all the crickets, when they were cricketing, sounded like a chorus of angels singing. So that's the relationship between time and self, and the human condition is going to do the same thing because the inner Buddha ones are all going to, in their golden form, we'll say, chime. It will be a tone that comes out from the bones and is broadcasted by the Buddha one in there as a self. That is how you are going to be recognized.

The clues to what your tone is are in the letters of your name. All the letters have musical valuation. You're going to find out that's what you are singing, or praying, as you walk. But you're not aware of it. As you become more aware of it, you become more attune with the space and the other entities in the same vicinity. You start singing like crickets! You recognize it, yet you won't be doing anything; you'll feel different.

Space will then begin to acknowledge you. You will be able to see at least one of the beings who has the capacity to manipulate space for you. As you work with this one, he or she will introduce others. So the groupings of you here are working with others shifting greater space, greater space. The presence requires peace first to all beings. Whatever is in that space, peace to all beings.

As the presence of peace everywhere begins to widen, you will get a nourishment you hadn't expected. Beyond that, I cannot say more. But you will have many who will be angry under the conditions of peace. You will find out who they really are. You will find out that there are such beings who mean to damage the human condition and the human spirit as well. You not only have the Holy Spirit with you but you have your own human spirit you are developing, like you are developing the next personality through your heart for your next incarnation, as it is to come. That is what you use for knowledge to get anywhere. It is what you use for understanding because you have gone through it.

People who have never been in a war have no idea — none, absolutely not. What you see in movies is not the same as it is in the actuality of it. You see all these refugees and what they are experiencing; their stories are horrific. It is not entertainment; it is not. There are those who are flabbergasted, in a manner, that this is occurring because they have heard the word "war" but then never heard it described in a descriptive way the victims of it are describing it now: parents and family members killed in front of them, chopped up with machetes while alive. All these horrific things are getting into the media now, not the normal news, but it is coming out.

It is going to create an issue when you find out who is really causing these wars. It is not the little guy who is causing these things. These things are instigated for a reason — for control of the planet, for the unification. The one who is going to stop all this war who is going to be, what you say, the hero thing. Political leaders don't understand who is perpetuating this nonsense. It is not ... well, it is in a way, so we can't say it isn't. Part of the religious structures you beings have developed along with your planetary system have caused more destruction than they have in the healing process of allowing life ever, and it is worse now. You are going through a wake-up call.

Beings in your United States of America have never been attacked by a foreign army in your country. They have no idea. Prayers will keep that from happening. Yet you have ones trying to instigate riots in your world and your country here, race wars, just to start something, because they don't have anything to do. They think by starting this, there will be something to do. The human condition has developed to a point where they are requiring everyone else to supply them with their needs. The things that built this foundation were the farmers. That's where the food came from, and you don't have any anymore. You have corporations poisoning you, and you know it.

Accomplishment versus Procrastination

The difficulty is the requirements for the spiritual self have been ignored. They have been ignored. The spiritual understanding of learning and comprehending and applying hasn't been applied here. Everyone talks about everyone else instead of doing something because at the end of the day, you need to feel in the body human a sense of accomplishment of what you've done for the day. So when you're working, no matter what it is, you take joy in doing it for the simple reason that later you will have a sense of accomplishment as you go into your sleep state, and you can wake up in the same presence on the planet, joyful to do something. You need to apply action through the physical form for the accomplishment of self. No one is going to tell you. You know whether you did anything worthy or not. That sense of accomplishment now is needed for the perpetuation of your own physical existence now, because if you're not accomplishing anything and you haven't done anything, then you're not worthy of further understanding.

Ants are worthy, the bees are worthy, the birds are worthy, the human condition was built to be worthy. But its worthiness now has turned into complaining instead of accepting the self-accomplishments of work that was done in the day. You did it. You made it through it and completed it. That is very important now just for the sense of the stability of the mind, which is behind you, getting to this point, so the brain that is present in you now can function in a manner that it is worth something. Why? Because it did something. Why? Because it did something. The brain participated in the ability to do something, and you put up your own arguments: "Oh, I will put that off till later." Who's talking there? It is not the one for your benefit, though you think it is when you can do it tomorrow because it gives you space that you can say, "Oh, okay." Then you don't do anything now, just like everybody else who is not doing anything. Then you go with the heaviness into your sleep because it wasn't done. It is a weight on tomorrow to do when you already have things that you are not aware of yet tomorrow that are going to be in front of you that will need to get done. So postponing is no longer an option, nor is it healthy. I'll tell you that much.

This is where you're going to understand what health really is. The reason you die and get sick is because you're lazy. You don't want to do anything. Eventually, you will get old and have this understanding of your transition, but that's different from the young stuff. Everybody wants this leisurely, highflying lifestyle of doing nothing. But your accomplishment is going to be found to be (how say you?) ... you will find in the passing of those who have done nothing that you are going to be grouped with others perhaps a little more arrogant than you in their condition of doing nothing, overlords of the lower realms. They are not fond of ones who accomplish. They are the ones who think they are the only ones who have the authority to authorize accomplishment. You are coming out of the change of the demons, if you let yourself understand that, that trap you with thought. It usually will be (how say you?) ... I do not want to give a particular direction on that. You will have to pick it up yourself.

There is an influence in the magnetics. Wherever you are, you know where north is, or you should have an idea. East, west, south — you have archangels stationed in each one of these positions. In the east is Raphael for healing, when the Sun comes up to heal your ignorance during the night. In the south, you have Michael who is the guardian of protection and protector of the realms. Gabriel you have in the west where the sun sets. Gabriel is the archangel, the leading one, of death, and he has a name with a list on it. That is why heart attacks occur during the night or early in the morning — because you are not accepting the healing of Raphael. As you go to sleep working with the energy of the west, you go running through the energy of the north, which is Archangel Uriel. He holds the gates of Tarsus, where souls try to escape the penance of this place, which is what you're going through, and then go to the other realms. Yet then you go down to the east with the Sun coming up on your planet for the healing of Raphael. You go through the cycle daily, daily, daily.

You should be thankful for the angels and their presence in the space so that you can have an opportunity to understand the grace of the space. You don't really understand how you even got here in the first place. But eventually you will, and eventually you will understand your purpose, which is more to save others than yourself or assist other souls and not just yourself or to be present in the space where it is needed just for you to be present. You don't have to say anything.

Be aware and adjust the space with your auric balance, your energy field. All auras are connected, and you just adjust. You think peace to all beings, and it starts. Then you are going to start being recognized by the "not so favorite" ones, we'll say. They will look to influence you, but you'll have to keep them at a distance right now. They know their places more than you do in the human condition. You are in that now. You are in the interaction between the physical world, the spiritual world, and the world of yourself — the world of yourself — which is the meditating one outside of you, beyond the death thing, beyond the death thing, into the presence of forever.

Water Provides Oxygen

When you understand the importance of water, that when you drink it, it's not just hydrating the body — as you like to say, "Put water in there to hydrate myself" — you are drinking it for the oxygen in there for your organs, for the oxygen in the water. You know how to transform it through the hydrolysis thing inside you with the chemical reaction that goes on. Your body breathes that oxygen because your nose and your mouth cannot bring in enough oxygen to feed your legs. It just will not get down there. It's the water and the pumping of the heart that supplies oxygen to the majority of the body. Your lungs supplied to the upper portion particularly, what you term, your brain function. Water is what all your organs acknowledge when you drink it. There is a thank-you there. You call it "quenching your thirst," yet it is appreciation from the beings in your body.

This is probably a phrase I shouldn't use because people might get confused by it. In each of your organs, there is a being, and they are learning to develop as beings. They know they came from the same place, so they consider themselves as relatives, you see. So you have a community of entities in you. They are your organs, but they came from the same place, the same force. They know they are relatives, yet the consciousness that you are working with creates spite and anger between the systems. The kidneys or liver has to handle this. The spleen has to handle this, modify it. They are all like an army trying to protect your heart from suffering. So if you understand this thing, you drink your water with a prayerful manner and thankfulness for assistance and aid to the systems inside you that are keeping you walking, but you think it is you. They are a compilation of yourself, all of yourself.

What you are going to find out is your stomach is in your hand. This is where that chakra goes — your stomach. This little finger here on the left hand is connected to your left leg. This finger here [middle] is connected to your right leg, and the thumb on your right hand is your will. So these are the organs you are working with, appendages actually. The stomach is in here [palms of hands]. The heart is right here [base of thumbs]. That's how they express themselves. This [index finger, right hand] is your right hand. This [middle finger, right hand] is your right leg. This [third finger, right hand] is your left hand; this is your left leg. This is you in your left hand, and that is your heart there.

He is going from the little finger to the thumb to the mount under the thumb.

Yes, that is why you put them together like this [put hands together in a prayerful manner] because in the right hand, there is the left hand, right here, energy-wise.

In the little finger?

Yes. In the left hand is the right hand (little finger). Right leg, left leg. So you put them all together like this [puts hands together and interlocks fingers]. Then you unify your etheric selves and your harmonious self, and the self that's you. You center this.

Hands together, finger to finger, thumb to thumb.

Then you take the tips of these fingers and put them under your chin, just to hold your head up. When you do that, you have an open palm thing. When you open your hand like this, your stomach is here, your stomach is here [in the palm of each hand], and you calm the stomach [massages palms together].

The being called Edgar Cayce has mentioned that all disease starts from the stomach. The processing of data, what's the data? It's the food you eat and the thoughts that you contemplate while you are eating it — all of that, all of that, all of it. Before you eat your food, you should say some prayers and thankfulness for the ones who grew it and the food itself for being grown for you. Yet most people don't. They don't want to understand the respect for a life giving you life. "Eh, it's just food; just eat it." But it had a life, and you're ingesting part of that life to keep you alive. So thankfulness is probably required, a little bit, in the essence of the dignity of your own self and what you're doing — not to influence anyone else, not to show off for anyone else. So you know what you are doing. It doesn't matter if they do or not. It doesn't matter because you have established communication with all of yourselves.

Your left self and your right self are linked together. You have seen the depiction in tarot cards of two little boys fighting each other. That's you. You grow up and become thankful for breath and water first. Then perhaps you learn how to grow something from the water that could sustain you so that you don't have to travel all over to get something. You should really be eating foods that are grown in your area if you know the consciousness of the area. Foods grown where beings are angry are not healthy foods to eat. They are not. Foods grown where beings are struggling and suffering just to grow are not healthy foods to eat because the thought process gets into the food. The food grows to balance that thought process and to even it out, and the food knows it. It is growing for that reason, yet that food is shipped somewhere else. It is not the same consciousness it was grown for.

You have gotten yourself into a quandary there, and right now, as these energies begin to shift, you're going to find your diets changing. Your diets are going to change. You're not going to be eating as frequently nor as heavily. There is going to be, we will call it, an electrical current. You'll feel it as an electrical current that will attempt to purify anything you eat. In that attempt, you might become disgusted with what you've just put in your mouth and have to eject it. There is another part of you, and this is for the human condition, to keep you alive longer so that you can understand it, and it can understand you.

So this is the importance of the Christ consciousness within your self. You've heard the name. You've heard the name. Everyone has heard the name. Some are claiming now to be Christ, threatening to kill some beings, actually have killed a being, because they would say that they were Christ. Obviously that's not the entity within the one. You're developing this understanding. This time in your world, you're seeing the insanity of all things. You're seeing it. It is there, and you're watching the result of it. You are watching the result of it. This is where the brain cannot understand a new function of itself because the visions are going to start increasing. The interpretation of the visions will cause confusion and perhaps insanity unless you know how to stabilize, and then stabilize the space. Everyone is being influenced by this.

A lot of beings have this understanding of proof. I don't think you want Archangel Gabriel proving himself or any of the others underneath his command. They know what they're doing. My suggestion is to focus on the east. Sunrise, be thankful for the Sun, we'll say, coming up, and also be thankful for the rotation of Earth so that you have a sunrise. Allow the energy of the Sun in the morning, particularly at six o'clock, to heal you. At six o'clock in the morning, whether you know it or not, there's a very, very slim opening of pure health that comes through. They call it the crack of dawn for a reason. So if you can expose your solar plexus to that, you will be healed, but you have to get it at that minuscule moment.

Sunup is at a certain moment. How many minutes on each side?

It's more like milliseconds.

So you have to be there at the moment? Is it like 6:42AM?

You should be there about ten minutes to six in the morning

until a little after six. Once it hits six, it is pretty much over because it builds, builds, and builds. Then the curtain opens and closes.

Okay, no matter whether the sun actually comes up at five or seven? It's the 6AM?

No, it's sunrise, at sunrise. But six will be the number to get you focused, okay? As you start getting into the winter months, it is going to be balanced, six and six. What will happen is once you get the first hit of sunrise, then you will get your timing. You'll be at the time of the Sun. I'm saying six so at least you'll say, "Well, the sun's already up," and then you'll get up earlier and earlier and get the crack [of dawn].

You will find this is part of the training where you learn how the Sun is leading you on the path of correctness and what you call the divine spark. The Sun is related to Archangel Michael, which is in the south. So at noontime, where generally the Sun is in the south area, or region, in your world, the direction, anyway, going to the west, there is another opportunity for expansion. But you must let the force of the Sun tell you, and pay attention to Archangel Michael on that one. You have to start communicating with the archangels on this thing here, or at least your angels, because they have jurisdiction and authority with what is beginning to happen. They don't ask questions. They don't particularly enjoy conversation, you say. They would rather work with ones who can feel the force and then send it out, as a mirror — come back and work with it.

The Amphibian Energy of the Human Condition

You will feel the telepathic ... I don't want to call it "telepathic" because that's what everyone else is doing, playing mind games. It's more of a synapse excitement in the brain of having discovered a new ability. The brain wants to, now, make a direct connection with the heart, and it drops down energy there. The heart wants to make a direct connection with the brain, and your mind holds background data because it's what you've done.

Now the brain and mind and heart want to reestablish, what is termed, a cognizant mind. So you will be everywhere, everywhen. You just turn the dial. Your mind becomes present with you and the brain, and you unitize consciousness with all the angelic beings. You will find out that you are much more than what you think you are. This is a time when self-judgment will start hitting you: "I should've done 'this.' I should've done 'that.'" Just back up. That's the mind thing. The brain purifies you. Drink water, and be thankful for it.

The significance of the self — your self, the you who is inside of you and is afraid to show itself to anybody else — is coming forward now, that you, the little you in there, the baby you that hid the minute you found out this was not a planet of love. Where did love go? You knew about it, then you found out it wasn't, and you hid in there. That one is coming out now, or wants to. It's willing to. It's getting the courage to peek. As it begins to peek, the heart expands, and there is another acknowledgment in there because this is what we call the secret one of your self, the one that has his private dreams, private space, that one. That's moving now, and when it does, it's going to be like a bunch of frogs coming out of the water all over the place chirping, chirping, chirping. Just let it chirp a bit and then calm it down.

The human condition has a lot of frog and amphibian energy in it. That magic of the frog is there, the ability to hide under the mud and in the water and then come out. That one is moving. It is not (what you say?) evil as some perceive and say. It is an education process of the deeper self of you. It is beyond the subconscious. It is what allows you to have a subconscious. It's your frog energy; we'll call it the frog energy, your amphibious energy, that form. Then you have the dragons coming up and out. Then you have the birdman working and walking, or starting to — with feathers on their legs. You have all these forms, body forms, that are part of you that you are not aware of yet how you, as you say, move space, but right now what we're working in this time; it is not the interior. It is an exterior force doing this. You haven't made those connections yet.

There is a propriety in this force because it can heal anything, anytime, anywhen. It just does it. It's a word that you beings call "miracles," but there are no such things as miracles, in a manner, if you understood them, how they're perceived to be. It's a shift of time, and we've told you that before. In order to heal an injury, you have to go back before it. You have to go through the pain adjustment, but even that can be changed. So when these miraculous healings start taking place, the acknowledgment has to come from within, not directed toward the one who provided the opportunity for it. The one who allowed the miracle was the you inside you if the healing was required. You allowed it. Pretty soon people are going to understand that they prefer life instead of the communication with this death process or confirmation of existence. The preference for life will produce life; that's what it does.

Life is life, no matter where you are. That is an understanding of change. You're not aware of that part yet. That is the difficulty going on now. You have a lot of beings committing suicide and thinking it's going to get better, but it is not. You go back at least two steps to figure out why you didn't understand. Suicide is not an option. You may think it is, but it isn't. It is not the place you want to be. You will be in a place with other suicides because it's the same consciousness, and that's not a comfortable position to be in. Everybody's whining. That's all they do is whine. "I can't do anything. I just want to whine." Wah, wah, wah, wah, whine, whine, whine. They have no clue. They haven't even been instructed, in a way, yet they knew before. They knew before.

This Time Frame Is to Experience Life

Many beings chose to experience this timeframe to experience life from other places, other dimensions, all those things. They are sorry they did because they didn't choose wisely, you say. You set a condition, you answer the call, and then you are sent. Basically, you are out there, and you hear a prayer. You pay attention to it, and it is significant to you for some reason. It doesn't matter. You sit there, and then you're sent as an answer to the prayer. So your being born was a miracle for your mother and an answer to her prayer, because that's how it works. Whatever prayer that was or whatever thought was going on there, a requirement of your self answered it. The responsibility for that is the process of growing up so that you learn to be careful about what you attach your attention to, out there and down here. Any questions?

Can you clarify the frog, the birdman, and the dragon? Are these energies or forms that we inhabited previously?

They are forms that you exercised with and inhabited previously, but they also come in to inhabit you now, to recognize you. As you get your dragon energy in there, just remember the force of the dragon. The frog energy, you are aware of. Frogs have a symbolism, a magic. You're aware of that, yeah? So this sort of magical knowledge is available to understand, and they teach that.

Oh, so they are going to teach us, the birds, the dragons, the frogs, if we are open?

Yes. It's not that you're it. You might feel like it, but that's part of their teaching modality to let you know who is teaching. If you have a frog energy, that's not you. It's an overlay that is instructing you in some way, in its natural intelligence. You see, it doesn't read books, doesn't need books. Those are the inner processes you're going to begin to work with — frogs, birds, dragons. Then you have ... well, that's the majority right now. Then you have other entities. You have the ant people, things like that. Those are the workers.

The human condition is going through all its changes, and it is going to learn, eventually, the compatibility of all nature with itself eventually — eventually. Right now you're having a mass genocide going on. It's worse than, what you term, when the Nazi Germany thing happened. It's not available from all your media yet. You have humans in positions who are running this and knowing it.

Humans?

Yes, and they are being influenced too. They know it. They think it's a power thing, but it is going to come to naught actually. The human condition has a difficult understanding that there is consciousness in nature and in space — and everywhere. This consciousness can affect everything and make it do things. It affects everything. You had a sandstorm over in Israel the past two days. You had a sandstorm, and [in Saudi Arabia,] an electrical storm knocked a crane off by lightning. It landed in one of the most holy mosques in the Muslim world; it crushed the house. It didn't hit the black cube there, but it wiped out 200 people or more. Fortunately that happened when it did because in the next two hours after, there was supposed to be 10,000 people there, but they didn't show up.

You're getting a battle here now. One of the warriors is nature. The human cannot win that one. So you need to understand who is behind nature, these natural forces that cause dust storms and thunderstorms and earthquakes. It's not just, what you call, a chemical reaction. These are emotional energies being stirred. You have more volcanoes going off in your world than you've ever had before. Now, just yesterday, there were eight inches of snow in Utah. It's only September. The weather's changing, and you're getting alterations in your poles, what you think is. Yet it is a magnetic influence being affected by molten lava and things and the planetary movements, of Nibiru coming around. All of this is influencing the consciousness of your self, but you're not aware of it. Pretty soon you're going to need to talk to the wind and ask for peace from the wind to stop it. It will stop. You're going to have to learn which one of you — is that the frog doing it? Is that the dragon doing it or the bird doing it? One of them knows how to do it.

Why are they doing it?

Increasing the native frequency calls, you mean? Nature is upset with the human condition. You have destroyed your forests, and now the bears are coming out of the woods into the community for food. Scientists cannot figure out why all of a sudden 60,000 antelope in central Asia just dropped dead in four days.

A plague. In another understanding — I'm going to have to phrase it this way because of the words — because God so loves the creatures here, instead of having them suffer the way the human condition is going to suffer, he's taking them out first, in large numbers. So the animals themselves do not have to suffer what is going to come into the consciousness of human. You think you are just two legs, two arms, and a head walking. They're much more than that. You haven't realized yet. You perverted it. That's why you don't want to realize it. You are going to be cleansed about it also. This is why you are going to find a lot of beings talking to a rock because that allows them something that is grounding that doesn't move.

There's another reason why you had pyramids built. They can't move. They can't roll. They are also picking up high frequencies now being here, what you would term, causing inner activation everywhere. Lights are coming out of the skies. "Those are portals," lightbeings like to say. But they are not so much portals for going up. They're portals for coming down. You may not like the appearance of the entities coming down because of your judgments. You thought "this" and, "This isn't what I thought it was going to be," type thing. The presence of your self hasn't been developed to be in the presence of itself — your self. That is what is happening now.

The intense discipline needed for instruction in the divinity of yourselves is not noticed because everyone's flying off in the ego of himself or herself. It never has to do with you. It always has to do with the greaterness of everyone else, really. This is the significance of the Christ frequency within the self. It's going to be called, and the only one who truly knows how to do it is the frog in you, the resurrection process thing comes out of hibernation. Then the bird will take over, and the dragon will be there. That is how it works.

The beings from Sirius have come. They are going to come through the center star of Orion, which is the Jerusalem Command. It's going to open. It is going to open. There will be a huge light that descends, and there'll be an enormous amount of energy available. I'll say that.

So that's a good thing?

That is a good thing. We are still trying to move a meteor

Figure 5. *Note the person in the lower left.*

from hitting this place. Now, there's only one way that I see it, and this has been discussed in many places to slow this down or to prevent it, actually. The meteor's moving, and Earth is moving. You can't stop the meteor. You might, perhaps, back up the rotation of Earth just a little bit, slow it, if you can. You can. You can. You can. Then as you understand the prayer to do that, you will understand the significance of, what you say, [taps] this being coming through because he is beyond the stars [see figure 5]. He is getting out, and he acknowledges it. You know it was there. Now he sees and can bring it through, both. He has the ability not to go back and forth like that. That is what you are doing now. Everyone's going through this. You have been mesmerized by this, and now you're coming out.

Once you get out into here in these realms, there are songs and tones. Then you bring it down for the benefit of others. You bring it down for the benefit of others. One of the things with healing … and the healing of the planet is going to take place overnight, actually. It will be quick. You won't even remember the sickness. But people have an issue with being sick. It's the way they attract attention to themselves. The organs are what are requiring the attention, not the external form. This is what is happening now in this understanding.

You Are Becoming

As you live in this time in reality, you are going through the participation of your death. You're living your death because, as you pass from this form, you'll go into a greater life. You don't realize that yet. The fear and the judgment constructs of being here is what creates the confusion. But the knowledge that you have a brain and the knowledge that you have a heart and the gift of a presence, nobody really knows what that presence is. You have a gift of presence. It's not just your body. It is not just your organs. There is a presence about you. Everybody knows something about it because you sense it, but you can't quite touch it.

That presence knows you very well. It has a manner of the One who is breathing you from all your skin, your pores. It does that. It breathes you through your skin or tries to. You are being introduced to that form, from our understanding, in the healthiest way possible. There is this damage that beings somehow enjoy doing to themselves. They think it's somehow self-satisfying, yet it isn't. It's causing damage to the systems. The inappropriate behavior, the inappropriate talk, the inappropriate foods — all of this is what does it. You think it is an escape, but it isn't.

What you are going to find in moments of need — by that, I

mean you'll be hungry — just the thought of food, any food, will satisfy the need. If you go for the food that you thought of and purchase it and cook it, you're going to find out you can't eat as much as you thought you could. You envision the whole thing, but you can only eat a little bit. So that is the training in the thought of the food to satisfy you. You'll still need water and some sustenance but not the mega amounts you thought you needed. So you are going to be trained, in a manner, in a different way to sustain the body with sustenance — lighter foods, lighter vegetables, water, and different contemplation. Even a different environment, where you eat, is going to be important.

You have to be very careful now. You're moving into an arena where you have openings in the astral. Some of those beings in there are not pleasant. They can't go up, and the only place they can go is down, and you're the down right now, because you are going up. They're going to try to influence you. "Do this up here; you're new here. You don't know how it goes. You're going up there, so let us show you how it goes." No! You got there. Keep going up. Go to the next one. Don't be entertained. Don't get on any merry-go-rounds. Don't. No! That's what happened this time. Don't be enthralled by the vision of it, the fantasy of it. That is another trick. It's like a lure for fish, and you get caught and you get stuck over there. Don't.

You Are in the Application of What You Know

Learn how to allow the right auricle of your heart to talk to you. It wants to. Then the soul of you in the heart can communicate, and the brain can start talking directly to the heart and get things done — get things done. You are in that other expression now, where you are becoming but you don't have to die to become. You become more, and then you use your mind and go back and do the healing process for your presence. It becomes a simple contemplation. Actually, it's a formula for self.

The partitions, we will have to say, are (some of these are your words, and they are not definitive enough) beginning to be brought down, taken away. Slides, I guess you call them, sliding doors. You're going to see beings there who have been watching you perform. They are there to congratulate you, in a manner. Some might not be as appropriate to you as they should be, but they are evaluators of your performance. This just happens to be the school you are in, and in the type of school you are in, the evaluations are different. In different schools, some are stricter than others. As you move up more into the definitive logic of your divinity, the stricter the better.

You are corrected quickly, so you don't have to live the lie and overcome it again. You accept the correction. That is the process that the human condition is in right now because it has been written about and written about and written about and written about. Now you're in the application of what you know. You either know what you know, or you don't. What you know is going to take you to your next opportunity. There is always an opportunity for improvement. So ask for strength, power, peace, and protection. You are going to need strength now. The bone is the entity that knows what strength is, and the consciousness that develops the muscles, tendons, and sinew knows the application to build more strength — walk, lift weights, exercise — but the bones know inherently what strength is. You ask for that strength to be sent to your systems.

Sometimes the life process has to be interrupted because you have gone too far on the wrong path. Your high self has asked permission for intercedence, and young people dying early is one of the reasons. Sometimes it's because they want just part of the experience, and they don't want the rest of it. You take a piece at a time, but that's not a human condition; it's a jurisdictional process. You're moving into jurisdictions now. The authority is coming. You can do this, or you can't. I'm talking spiritually speaking. This is going to upset a lot of people because everyone right now is in a battle with telepathy. They're playing telepathy games, mind games, and all the stuff. When you beings figure this out, you're not going to like it. Eventually you will move above it because you have accepted it, you see. You don't have to accept it. You don't have to accept it.

One of the secrets — real, real secrets — of longevity in this world is drink water sacredly. At times, you probably should just not let anyone see it. Write on it, communicate directly with the water, with the hearts fervent intent, and be thankful for it, especially before you go to bed. Then when the sun comes up, you will see what happens. You're a new being, actually, a new being, because the process of self-forgiveness occurs during the night when you sleep. That is something you should do. Forgive yourself every night before you go to sleep. Get ready to start the day again by doing something because if you don't do anything, you're not worth anything. I don't consider a lot of talking doing something. You most likely can tell what you need to do when you want to postpone it right there, right there. That is what you need to do.

We are through.

CHAPTER

12

The Envelope of Your Life

September 22, 2015

This session, this little time now, has to do with what is going to be termed the envelope of your life. You were born with an intent, number one, to be born and to be expressed. That's what you are doing now — walking around, talking. The divine part of your being that manifested you through the sperm and the egg (the consciousness around it, the development of it), your intent was there, an intent, an intent. That intent was the understanding of moreness, because in previous lifetimes, you've died. You "played die," and you had another chance. You term it, incarnation, eh? But it's focused intent. You are always alive somewhere — peace to all beings! — and the soul of you knows this.

The hearts now are starting to awaken. They are going to speak. As we have said before, the hearts are going to speak, yet you don't understand the nature of the heart. You think that's where love is. It's not; it's the soul. The heart speaks vile things; it's desirous. It wants, it wants, it wants, and it wants. It claims, "Mine, mine, mine." That's why we have said the brain is present. Your mind is behind you. You've done it; that's why you know something. You've gone through it. Whether it is right or wrong, it doesn't matter. You had the expression, experience, of it.

The consciousness now on your planet is going through the understanding of what intent is; that's why all this war thing is there in front of you. So your heart is going to speak, but you must now remember you are a conscious entity with a brain present now, and you're going to choose a forward motion with the heart in accompaniment, not arguing. This is the unification of the left and right sides of the brain. You take lavender flame, and you run it through there [sewing the left and right sides of the brain together] — Saint Germaine's authority. It unifies the consciousness that's involved with using the synapses of your brain to transfer information down to the divine self of you, which has to include every organ: liver, lungs, kidneys, heart, lymphatic system, all your fluids. You are 70 percent water, or 60.

God's path (the word "God," the entity, form, intent of you) is through the water. It's through you; it's always through you, always, always, always. And in the manifestation process, which is what metaphysics was, a step to teach (1) that it's possible, (2) the calling forth, and (3) the reception. You are in that process now.

Soon you will understand that your oceans are not subject to, what you term, the tidal forces of the Moon, but they are the ones that are causing the Moon to move the oceans. The entity that moves through the water, the invisible force, it cannot be seen, and it moves everything from this pristine environment — Earth. That simple story of Adam and Eve, that's the heaven thing you're in at this level of consciousness. You breathe in God every day, or the life force that provides you life, eh? And it's the intent of your self — the interior portion — in a desirous expression that comes forth. Now is going to be the time to calm the heart because the heart has been spoken. It speaks vile things. It thinks it is the only one, that it deserves more. It does deserve more, but the communication has not been appropriately taught, we'll say. But it really should be understood as appropriately remembered, because you all remember you did it! When you were a little one walking around, crawling, you knew things, and you knew how to manipulate, or you tried to. You knew. You knew, and you grew up in the knowing of not.

You Are Moving Into the Consciousness of Acceptance

You have to get into the understanding that your pristine self is with you when you sleep, when you go to your safe chambers, we'll call them. You need to use a prayer (pick one, an earnest one) before you lie down. When you are in the synchronization of this, in the timing of (what you term) your planetary forces that are inscribed on your back in your horoscope, and when your mental capacity can understand that influence that's coming through your back, that's the spiritual forces from the planets you came through: Jupiter, Mars, Neptune, all of the spiritual entities that you signed contracts with. That's how you got the astrological chart; they are breathing you. That's why now you are starting to feel [inhales deeply] this breath. It wasn't yours. Where did that come from? That's the recognition in the physical form — reaction — of a holy presence entering you.

Now you have to calm the self down and move back into the spine. The bones are your most important resonance factor in the communication with the Divine. Your original tone, your tone, (manifested fetus, bones) is in the bone. Your intent is in your bones. The sheath around your bone is the clothing of the Holy Spirit that compresses the bone, little bit, squeezes it to create the blood and the marrow, that pumps it through your heart, so that the body can have an expression called life as you walk with it.

This force is making itself known. The inside communication

— this is the most difficult part for the human condition — is to pay attention to the inside of you, not just the heart, because you are going to hear some vile things, selfish things. It hasn't understood the compassionate nature of itself for power. You start using your brain process, synapses, and work further in the crown chakra to find your purposeful intent because you are meditating out there, and you are down here as a result of your meditation — the whole group, everyone. This is that synchronization process that is starting to go on.

When this journey of the concept of oneness starts, you are going to have a panic attack. When you move into oneness, that is all that's there: just you, no one else, no one else. You are alone in a white cloud in oneness. Then the loneliness of self (because you need other reflective forces to understand your true self) descends, out of the [state of being] lonely, in a manner, for acceptance — acceptance in the manner that there are other beings there, reflecting forces back and forth. So in that reflection process, you understand it metaphysically. But in the reflection process, you understand your intent also and the power behind space. Space is what has allowed you the grace to grow.

The space that you are living in and walking in, her name — it is an entity — she is called Grace. As you walk through her, with her, you're showing your understanding and respect, as you would interpret it for the entity, a supreme being, called Grace, just by the way you act and move. She knows it, and the other divine beings know it. You are in a practice mode now. You are in practice, and you are practicing to find out what your intent is and was not involved with karma. That's another game to get you to play, but your true intent of the self of you, your self — the self that answered a prayer for the union of the sperm and an egg — whatever prayer it was.

You agreed in the manifestation, the performance of the pleasure of the parents' actions. You came walking forth as a result of it. Now, if the parents understood, or understand, the wisdom and things without the manipulation forces, they would see the proud condition of a birth of one. Yet the consciousness in this country [United States] is not set that way. The privilege of birth, the privilege of being a parent, the privilege of being a mother, and the privilege and understanding of being a father — there are different frequencies involved there. There is intent involved in the learning process of your self, called the expression of life. Are you worthy to continue the perpetuosity of it, to continue it not only for yourself but also for others? It requires a protection of space, protection of space, in your words "protection of space." It's a cleanliness in your auric field, a sensitivity in your layers of perception — when to stop a thing moving in your direction or back up.

You are learning that you are in traffic now, spiritual traffic. A lot of beings are trying to get your attention, and the moment you go (that way), instead of figuring out the intent of you, God is moving through you, because you are water, and it's path is through the water.

The inner communication now is extremely important. You are going to need to reassure your organs that you love them, because they are assisting you — the stomach, the heart, the lungs, the liver, and the kidneys, the whole system of self. You are going to find out that there are entities in there, and there is going to be speech coming up from inside you as the organs get their, I'll say, authority to speak with permission for the education of the consciousness called the human condition. But you have to listen to it. It's the type of talk that is different from the sound of the human voice. It has a harmonic in it, and it also sometimes will feel as if all the organs want to speak at once, and you say, "Slow, slow."

You are moving, the human condition now is moving, into a consciousness for the acceptance, an acceptance, of their own selves as being privileged entities in understanding the perpetuosity of life and the continuity of it for all things. In other words (we'll put it another way), you are moving into your god form with permission. As that permission is granted, you get more authority over the conditions within the system called your self for the protection of the species that was set here — all species, all of life walking differently from invisible. All of it is connected.

The Secret of Water

There is a force that is jealous of the human condition. It does not think it deserves to be in the position it is in because it was not one of the first creations, no, or existences, we'll say — matter. That force works against you. Yet when you understand the privilege that you have within the self of you, then you understand the true power that you have available to you because of the envious nature of this other entity. He is aware of that power that's coming to the human condition for those who understand the beauty, the divinity, and the sanctity of simply the water moving through you — this beauty, the simplicity, and the wonderful nature of breath through you, as you breathe moment to moment.

The other conditions, other entities (we call them conditions; you call them entities), they don't have the opportunity to understand what breath is: [inhales] calling in God and releasing [exhales] what does not belong and the cleanliness of the interior portion of the being. Too often you breathe [inhales] and say things you wish you hadn't said later on. So in the breath, now, you are going to start learning these things. Each nostril provides the meridians in your system with different frequencies. The left nostril brings up, what you call, portions of the interior self. The right nostril brings up portions of the exterior idea of self, exterior idea of self. The water you drink provides the oxygenation for the systems within the body. It is not just water to bathe and shower in inside. The organs extract the oxygen from it [water] down to your toes. The bones pull the oxygen out of it [water] as it runs through the lymphatic system; it has a suction effect. The water cries for the oxygen, just as you do. [Inhales.] The water gets it into your system.

Now, the secret of the water, since God's path is through the water (put a name on this God thing if you have to or not; it's the same being). Its path is through the water. And since it is, if you write on the water, contemplate the water before you drink it, just a blessing to the self, not gulping the thirst and things, "Ah," but consciously think of. You don't even have to write on the water. You can visualize thoughts on the water. The understanding is that there the system is healed.

You are in a time now where you can understand the miraculous nature of things by just calling forth a presence, a presence, a presence. The strongest and most comfortable presence you can call right now in your genetic understanding in the continuity of your self being on this planet is your grandmother, your mother's mother, your mother's mother, your mother's mother. She knows what suffering was — is — because she went through it. Yet she responds in the happiness nature as you say a prayer with her or for her, as you in that genetic line. She has this energy of feeling proud of the little one who's there still working. There's a connection in that genetic line, and being here — you, the one — you're the knot that knows this, and it helps straighten the line. So everyone in your genetics can start breathing easier without the judgment things, and in a condition of what you call humanity, a communal sense starts taking place.

You see the need for others because you can't do everything, and everyone has a specific — specific — divine design, unique only unto you. It's like a gear of a great cosmic clock. As the gears become acknowledged, we'll say, in mechanical understanding, they link and then the great clock turns, and the great consciousness expands. What you call the selfishness of self's self — me, me, me, me, me, me, me, me — blends into a communal thing of compassion and support for the system called space, because if you didn't have space, you would not be walking around. If you did not have your bones, you would not be walking around, and if you did not have the intelligence of the synapses or the movement of you (and the muscle and the sinews connecting with the bone and all your overlays and all your stuff), you wouldn't be moving anywhere.

Humans Are Worthy

Now I am going to say a thing. You are seeing births come into this planet, now, through systems, and they are not in a good condition. That's because the procedure and the conception process were not … the procedures were not adhered to — delicacy, decency within nature in the process of conception in the forming of a human condition. It asks for permission and prayers to bring forth one. But how often is that done? You even have your churches now, these things coming through with this pedophilia thing. Why? Because the young ones know and the old ones want them to forget and [and the old ones want to] control things. It's out there now. It's out there; it's in the media. Yeah! Everybody is getting rights now; you're going to want your pedophiles to have rights. Well, good for you. You are going to learn something through this little nonsense.

The jurisdiction of the Grace of space is going to be acknowledged. In other words, there is going to be a correction.

There is going to be a correction. You have your wars; you have your arguments within your individual churches and things. There is no one, anyone, to really look up to anymore, and in your biblical understanding, you know of this thing called the antichrist coming. Well, when you find out that nobody is looking at anybody and the being just wants to be there, guess who that is? Then what are you going to do? You are going to find that this being really exists. Then what? You haven't developed your own understanding of the power of self to contain that force that tries to influence you and control you — and not for your greater good, either.

"Peace to all beings" is going to be, what you call, a concept that will be understood, because that's an entity who moves, and the place he moves is peace. He creates it, creates it, because he has a shock affect on the heart and the solar plexus. He has the ability to turn it off, off. He works with the Archangel Gabriel, who is the angel of the Moon, who understands the waters, and he is the lead angel of death with the book of names. Those entities are real. So is Michael, so is Raphael, and so is Uriel. They are the ones working and willing to instruct, if you pay attention, in the consciousness called the human condition in the United States of America. You have other concepts. You have the pagan things. You have this witchcraft thing, dark forces, and pleasure. It's molasses.

The water is the life. The water is the light. There is an invisible force that moves through the water and unifies things, brings things together, brings things together for the enlightenment of the human condition as a unit within the self — your self — not that you are better than anyone else, no. It gets heavier in the understanding that you are going to need more compassion because they don't know. They don't know, and you are going to see soon, sad to say, beings falling on their knees crying, just overwhelmed with the abuse that is going on. Then the assistance will be given to overcome this, because the hearts are not what you think they are in the intent, in the avenue, and in the action that's being applied now.

There used to be cockles on the heart — warm, fuzzy, little feelings — looking at everything. But the human condition has pretty much destroyed that now, because there is no joy for the heart to look at anything. The heart is now complaining about everything, and when it speaks, you are going to hear it. You are going to hear it, and then you are going to feel the self, the need of correction within the self, "How can I help this heart?"

You have four beats there, four chambers. In the center where they all meet is the cave, a little hidden cave where your light spark exists. It is so frightened to come out because of the ignorance of the condition it sees around itself that it stays there. That connection, now, is going to start taking place with the soul, with its power, because the soul wants to leave, but now it's deciding to stay. And with the synapses of the brain being present now, you know about the soul. You know about the heart. The three of you can work together.

The brain is an entity. The brain is an entity or, you call it, a computer, but it's an entity. It knows how to think really quickly, so to speak. I don't mean think; it processes data. It processes the visual experience that you can't see. That is what it does from, what you call, the way down in you. Now those three beings are going to start working, but they're incorporated in you. It's the brain, which is present, the soul, which is in the solar plexus, and the heart. They are going to unite. That's your trinity. That's *your* trinity.

Then you have an expression (how you say?) of a flower opening. Well, your soul is here [makes a pyramid shape at the chest]. The base is across here [points beneath the breast at the solar plexus], and the apex is at the throat. What is going to happen is this portion here at the throat is going to go up above the head, the base is going to drop below the feet, and you're going to be standing there as a gold lightbeing, in a manner, or sitting there. Then this apex is going to open up [exhales], come down, and form an apex below you. That calls your genetic line together for the healing of the consciousness unit, units, from where you came from. It proves that someone along that line did it, and when that happens, there's a, you term it, family reunion going on. There are others before you who have done this, and they are waiting for you to understand it.

You are part of this worthiness of self is what we are trying to get into the understanding of the human condition, not better than anyone. Worthy, yes, of all things, and then you understand how the intent brings those to you. You don't damage anyone, don't harm anyone, peace to all beings, because you know at times with ones there is a despair that can't seem to be lifted. But it can be, and when you understand the magic of your fingers, these two particularly [holds up index and middle fingers], you bring those across your heart. The heart knows what these two fingers mean. It does. Simply touching it, you feel a difference, an acknowledgment of your inner self to the outer self.

You Are Here to Help Balance the Interior Portion of Beings

Now allow me this understanding. You take these two fingers [holds up the index and middle fingers of the right hand] and just put them over here [points to the heart], just a little bit inside. Feel yourself feeling the thankfulness for the self, and that little moment of feeling should be up here in the crown chakra. You felt it. Those are the signals that truly exist from another dimension somewhere. Well, you are here, you think, for yourself, but you are *really* here for someone else because you said you would do it. You are on, pretty much, a spiritual rescue mission, whether you know it or not. Yeah, and you succeed every day, yet you don't know that.

There is a limitation now on what selfishness is going to bring, and the desires and understanding of moreness is what the heart really yearns for in what, you would term (how you say?) … you're just relaxing in a warm bath. In the human physical condition, your heart wants to be that, inside the physical form, you. It just wants to relax there and move with it instead of under the struggle things. Now, what has confused the heart has been the mind. You forgot that you are present. If you're already done, that's past. Present — next! Then you accumulate wisdom of the Grace of the space because you have the ability to move. Simply turning in a circle will change the auric energy you are receiving, will change the auric energy you're receiving.

The entity you call Jesus has no animosity toward anyone; everyone has it toward him. The abilities displayed by that one are available for everyone, it has been said. But you can't take credit for it as from yourself, because it flows through you; it goes through you. It is like that being who speaks through your back that comes in there. That's the Holy Spirit, Shiva, who does that, just introducing himself. It comes out of nowhere. When you feel that, acknowledge it. Understand who Shiva is, what his (how you say?) mysteries are, because you're all in this mystery now — not the mystery of another self, but the mystery of your own self, own self.

You are here to help balance the interior portion of beings so that they feel comfortable, and they even allow an ability to express, because so often (particularly with the ones who are shut down, ridiculed, put down, dah-da-dah) they are put in the systems. But each country has different consciousness groupings, and you're finding out this Babel thing, what happened. In your world, your United States of America was given what would be understood as the gift, the ability, of more freedom of expression, allowance for it, than other places, anywhere. Now, your country's consciousness is being attacked because there are no defenses there for it in the consciousness understanding. By that, I mean prayers, appropriate prayers, prayers. Prayers defend. Prayers defend. Prayers defend.

Jesus was David. David received and gave the psalms. Jesus was Jesus on the mountain, and he reduced 150 psalms to the Lord's Prayer with pauses. Basically, "Our Father" (contemplate) "who art in heaven" (contemplate). He reduced 150 psalms to that form. It works.

If you do the pieces, you will find one piece that will stand out for you, or to you, actually. "Oh!" Relegate that to your library of important insights because it creates a resonance in your bone that remembers where the bones came from before, before there were bones, before there were bones, before there were bones — before there were bones in any creature.

You are living a memory, literally, of the interior beauty of yourself and processing the data as your ability to accept that from yourself without the criticism of self because that inner beauty always wants to come forth. It doesn't need to be, as ones want to be adored and all of this thing and the ego thing. No! The inner beauty just wants to be allowed to be the inner beauty, regardless of anyone else. It just wants to be the inner beauty, and the outer beauty will understand the inner beauty.

Then you will have your presence, your own presence, your own, your own. When you start working with your own presence, you're going to find out that you'll be in new company, because your presence won't fit in with some other presences. It just won't.

Don't worry about it. Just recognize it, and allow yourself to move gracefully to another space, what you call, allow the space to change, because what is happening is the space is changing. That's why the personalities are changing. They'll want to be a little gentler now because something else is happening, I think.

People will say, "Did you feel the energy today? How was it, yesterday?" It's increasing. Your awareness is increasing. Your breathing patterns are going to change. You are going to start breathing from this chakra up here [points to sockets of the shoulders], and there are two chakras down here (right at the base where your lungs are). Down at the bottom there, there are two little ones. You are going to start using those as accessory air tanks, we'll say. You have a blowhole, like a whale, in the back here, right in the center of your astrological chart, that's going to open. You won't have a choice. Your back will go like that. It will open. The soul will start opening. You'll breathe that breath. It'll be another sort of graduation process, because when that breath hits, it comes up and enlightens the mind. A gold energy will flow right up there, and your cares and your little troubles that you thought were so extensive will go right away.

Youth today have the advantage of the significant understanding — of the significance — of the breath and the water incorporated in the body. Those are the prayers. Those are the prayers — breath and water, breath and water, breath and water, breath and water. Everything else will be given. Everything else will be given. When you understand, say, "Thank you for the breath," pray for the water, and watch what happens. Watch what happens.

There is a king of the water. He's called Liba, and Bafafes is prince of the waters. There are forty-two ministers who control the waters — all waters, little rivers, lakes, streams, oceans — and there is an entity called the Queen of the Sea. These forces are moving now. These forces ... you are getting princes and kings, literally, of the natural kingdom, nature, the elemental kingdoms. They know they are princes. They know they are kings, and they make nature move — the air, the earth, the water, and the fire. You have one other element, one other that's significant for the human condition, and that's wood. The trees are what are going to save you, because they show you how to transform negative energies into oxygen so that it can be breathed by others. That's what trees do. That is why some of them are so crumpled. You have, we will term them, demonic spirits that enter trees, for the feeling of life, movement. Then they come out. There is some education process going on there, and you're breathing their influence. So you are connected with all things.

Your wisdom, now, is going to be understood by the feelings in your back, the appreciation of nature and the natural forces, and the dignity of your own self in the skin and flesh that you are because you have earned it. Now it's time to realize it. It's a gift given, because you do not know how you did it. But you were involved in the doing of it. You were. You accepted and entered. You accepted and entered and said you would do, and you're doing it, reluctantly at times. That's why there are so many suicides going on now. The other one is trying to influence you. Don't [let it]! It is in the breath and the water — breath and the water, forgiveness of self, forgiveness of others, breath and the water, breath in the water, breath and the water, breath in the water — because when you drink the water, the oxygen is giving your system, body, form.

Peace to all beings! Allow your spines to be erect now, because we're going to adjust some energy here, as you wish. Peace down the crown. Let it come down the crown, go down to your pelvic area.

Peace to all beings. Peace to all beings. Peace to all beings. Peace to all beings. The energy in the stomach, push it down. Push it down.

There are several ways of getting rid of negative energy. You can throw it out, throw up; you can have gas and burp it up, or you can have gas and come out the other end. That is a form of expression that's going on in there that wants manifestation. You don't need it in there — in you. Push it out. Peace in the palms of your hands. This is where your stomach is, in there. Your will is here [points to the thumb], and when you're using the Lord's Prayer, the "Thy will be done" thing is involved there. So notice the energy that comes in your thumb when the "thy will be done" is said by you. Does it hurt? Is it pleasurable? Do you understand the connection? That's how you know where your will is. This [points to the thumb] is your own divining rod, and the will follows your genetic line, actually, and the perpetuosity of the condition called you — the family name (if you will) thing, because there is wisdom there.

Your genetic line survived those times so that you could be present now. There is an appreciation that's required at some level. You didn't do it. Thankfulness is required, thankfulness, to remember your mother and your father thankfully, not a judgment thing — her mother, her father, your mother's mother, mother, mother, her mother, her mother, her mother, her mother. All the mothers suffered more than you are doing now in the feminine condition. The males, they had an arrogance, every one, the power thing. And you're learning. That is what's going on now, and you are seeing it.

Prayers Are Needed Now

The only thing that is going to calm the situation in this, what you call space of your world, is prayer — the only thing, the only thing!

The higher you go, the more powerful the prayer comes, and then the spiritual leaders will have to start to listen because that is what is influencing your world now.

You have false spiritual leaders in power structures, and the pedophiles have rights, now. Where does that leave you? How could those conditions come about, the rape and torture of children? It's not a condition called principalities or respect. It is sick … sickness. It is beyond that. It's evil, because they know the little ones know. It hasn't really hit the mainstream yet, in the notification of it. But you're aware of it. It's going to, because everyone has justification for his or her own self, right? You are in that process now, entities.

Prayers are needed not only for you but for the space you are in and for those who don't know. The best prayers are the ones you do without telling anybody you did them. You find and you work with the ones that have results. I suggest Psalm 6. It's a short one. It has some very intense energies in it. It asks in the last verse that all your enemies be ashamed. It doesn't say to hurt them, and it doesn't just mean physical. It means especially in the astral for those who are attacking you, whether you don't know it or are aware of it. Ask for them to be ashamed, because shame is the one thing out there that no one — none — wants to participate with because everyone has it. It's a meltdown process.

Psalm 6 is strong, and verse 10 is stronger. First you have to forgive your own iniquities. That's the first verse. But when you work through it, you will see a profound effect on your environment because now people are being more attuned to the spiritual forces that are coming. At some level, they are. They are being affected. That's why you have so much demonic displays going on in your movies. That is what it is. You know it. It's fun, but it is a condition of consciousness that causes disease.

You are here because you said you wanted to perpetuate life and the understanding of love of God. Pick a name. The divine influence is invisible and for everyone. You are in this place, particularly in this state called Arizona, for spiritual reasons, whether you know it or not, because this state is going to be the center of major healing conditions, pretty much. Eventually, beings will come here just to walk into the boundaries of this area to be healed without touching or talking to anyone. The healers are going to abound; they will just be walking around, and everybody will feel it. But Arizona has already been declared that, or at least a section of the Southwest United States has been declared a healing region, and it means spiritual healing. It doesn't mean "fix my cut." It's a spiritual process because you are the healer of your self. You are. You are the ones doing it. You just forgot.

Call In Domes of Protection

Okay. Palms up to receive. When your palms are up, you are receiving blessings from the Father, the Mother, and your divine heritage. Call in your guides now, call them with permission to speak, those of you who understand what's going on inside you, for the heart to be understood appropriately for you and for the health and longevity of your body, for the health and longevity. Peace to all beings.

All right, movement now. I want you to think of your kin, your children if you have them, wives, husbands, boyfriends, cousins, aunts, and uncles. You want to call in, with permission, domes of protection around each and every one, domes of protection around each and every one, domes of protection, little domes of protection, so there can be self-reflection and appreciation for the space. Peace to all beings.

Anyone in your family who has a serious illness right now, I want you to focus on the name and the consciousness of that one, and we pray. We're going to bring our prayers together. I know you don't know what I am doing, but we're going to bring our prayers together for their supplication. Ask for permission for the healing and the health and the surprise introduction, the gifts, of Spirit.

Peace to all beings and mercy for ones who have confused minds. They need to know that the brain is present. The brain is in front. Peace to all beings. The unification of the brain and the heart stabilizes the system called the self, and the soul has an opportunity to appreciate the moment. Health to body, mind, and spirit. Peace to all beings.

Okay, palms together, if you will. Palms together. This gesture of palms together is the unification of the left side and the right side of your being. It's also the unification of your brain process as a unified brain. In the middle, there is a ball of light between your palms. Whether you see it or not, it's there. There is a conscious connection going into your solar plexus. That's what happens there. It's like you have your precious self between your two hands, but you don't know it, and that's why when you see it in the Buddhist tradition, they bring it up here [points to forehead]. There is a thankfulness to the head, pretty much, right there, palms up.

Now, bring in more space, more frequency. Bring it down, down, down, down, down. You see, no one really knows who anyone is yet. Health to body, mind, and spirit. Strength to the being. Strength to body, mind, and spirit. Strength to body, mind, and spirit, and the strength comes from the planet. Strength to body, mind, and spirit.

Peace to all beings. We are through.

Thank you very much.

Appendix

Psalm 147
Young's Literal Translation

147 Praise ye Jah! For [it is] good to praise our God, For pleasant — comely [is] praise.

2 Building Jerusalem [is] Jehovah, The driven away of Israel He gathereth.

3 Who is giving healing to the broken of heart, And is binding up their griefs.

4 Appointing the number of the stars, To all them He giveth names.

5 Great [is] our Lord, and abundant in power, Of His understanding there is no narration.

6 Jehovah is causing the meek to stand, Making low the wicked unto the earth.

7 Answer ye to Jehovah with thanksgiving, Sing ye to our God with a harp.

8 Who is covering the heavens with clouds, Who is preparing for the earth rain, Who is causing grass to spring up [on] mountains,

9 Giving to the beast its food, To the young of the ravens that call.

10 Not in the might of the horse doth He delight, Not in the legs of a man is He pleased.

11 Jehovah is pleased with those fearing Him, With those waiting for His kindness.

12 Glorify, O Jerusalem, Jehovah, Praise thy God, O Zion.

13 For He did strengthen the bars of thy gates, He hath blessed thy sons in thy midst.

14 Who is making thy border peace, [With] the fat of wheat He satisfieth Thee.

15 Who is sending forth His saying [on] earth, Very speedily doth His word run.

16 Who is giving snow like wool, Hoar-frost as ashes He scattereth.

17 Casting forth His ice like morsels, Before His cold who doth stand?

18 He sendeth forth His word and melteth them, He causeth His wind to blow — the waters flow.

19 Declaring His words to Jacob, His statutes and His judgments to Israel.

20 He hath not done so to any nation, As to judgments, they have not known them. Praise ye Jah!

Psalm 148
Young's Literal Translation

148 Praise ye Jah! Praise ye Jehovah from the heavens, Praise ye
Him in high places.
2 Praise ye Him, all His messengers, Praise ye Him, all His hosts.
3 Praise ye Him, sun and moon, Praise ye Him, all stars of light.
4 Praise ye Him, heavens of heavens, And ye waters that are
above the heavens.
5 They do praise the name of Jehovah, For He commanded, and
they were created.
6 And He establisheth them for ever to the age, A statute He
gave, and they pass not over.
7 Praise ye Jehovah from the earth, Dragons and all deeps,
8 Fire and hail, snow and vapour, Whirlwind doing His word;
9 The mountains and all heights, Fruit tree, and all cedars,
10 The wild beast, and all cattle, Creeping thing, and winged bird,
11 Kings of earth, and all peoples, Chiefs, and all judges of earth,
12 Young men, and also maidens, Aged men, with youths,
13 They praise the name of Jehovah, For His name alone hath
been set on high, His honour [is] above earth and heavens.
14 And He exalteth the horn of His people, The praise of all His
saints, Of the sons of Israel, a people near Him. Praise ye Jah!

Psalm 149
Young's Literal Translation

149 Praise ye Jah! Sing ye to Jehovah a new song, His praise in an assembly of saints.

2 Israel doth rejoice in his Maker, Sons of Zion do joy in their king.

3 They praise His name in a dance, With timbrel and harp sing praise to Him.

4 For Jehovah is pleased with His people, He beautifieth the humble with salvation.

5 Exult do saints in honour, They sing aloud on their beds.

6 The exaltation of God [is] in their throat, And a two-edged sword in their hand.

7 To do vengeance among nations, Punishments among the peoples.

8 To bind their kings with chains, And their honoured ones with fetters of iron,

9 To do among them the judgment written, An honour it [is] for all his saints. Praise ye Jah!

Psalm 150
Young's Literal Translation

150 Praise ye Jah! Praise ye God in His holy place, Praise Him in the expanse of His strength.

2 Praise Him in His mighty acts, Praise Him according to the abundance of His greatness.

3 Praise Him with blowing of trumpet, Praise Him with psaltery and harp.

4 Praise Him with timbrel and dance, Praise Him with stringed instruments and organ.

5 Praise Him with cymbals of sounding, Praise Him with cymbals of shouting.

6 All that doth breathe doth praise Jah! Praise ye Jah!

About the Author

Arthur Fanning attended the University of Rhode Island. After graduating, he entered the U.S. Marine Corps in the officer candidate program and earned his navy wings at Pensacola Naval Air Station in Florida. In 1968 and 1969, he served as a marine helicopter pilot in Vietnam.

Arthur had many experiences as a child in which he left his body and talked with beings in the stars at night. When he was a medevac pilot in Vietnam, the real nature of these experiences began to reveal themselves as a guiding and guarding force.

In 1986 he had what he calls "the big one" in his spiritual awakening when an entity appeared over Arthur's bed while he was still awake. Arthur's body lifted off the bed, bent in half, straightened out horizontally, and then lay back down, all in less than two seconds. There was no pain involved nor was it frightening. Arthur says, "It just happened. It felt like white electricity." Since then Arthur has been channeling and working with the entities who speak through him.

THROUGH ARTHUR FANNING

Soul Evolution Father

"Some of you are part of a great grouping that holds this universal system together simply by the thought, simply by allowing it to exist, and you're participating within it to assist in awakening (your word here). You are that in love with this experience and all things that are going on here. I'll give you a clue. You have succeeded in creating the shift. Now others upon your planet are coming to the awakening, for you let them do this thing their way. It is time for you to do more now, another thing: You term it 'healing,' only it's not that simple. Yet it is, for it would be termed a healing, because when the light understands itself, it understands the light of the other, and it is not really a healing. It is a remembering — the other remembers its power. That is how it works."

— Lord God Jehovah

$12.95 • Softcover • 208 PP. • 978-0-929385-33-4

Simon

It is with the book *Simon*, we brought his future self to his self at that time. We showed him to the beach and told him that everything is going to be okay because he was having concerns about life in general. As this process began to unfold, this channeling process, he was taken in dream state to places in the oceans and caves where the whales took him, he and saw crystals. There was this angelic being who accompanied the consciousness on the boat and was teaching him out of the body experiences. This is basically what this story is about in the dream state — of how to come back and go back and still be on a boat. So it gave him the confidence to continue the channeling.

Even in your Egyptian myths you see the boat of RA; that's very significant in the idea of crossing the river of death and coming back. You need a boat. So the concept was delivered in this book *Simon*. It will help ones in their inner passages, basically. It is a future self coming back to help the present itself.

$9.95 • Softcover • 64 PP. • 978-0-929385-32-7

TO ORDER PRINT BOOKS

Visit LightTechnology.com, Call 928-526-1345 or 1-800-450-0985,
or Check Amazon.com or Your Favorite Bookstore

THROUGH ARTHUR FANNING

The Comprehension of the Holy Spirit within the Human Condition

The spiritual forces within the self have been neglected, causing a lot of difficulty. In this series of channelings from the Spirit of Space and Gabriel et al. through Arthur Fanning, you'll learn how to acknowledge, respect, and make the most of these spiritual forces as you continue to work toward ascension.

Discover the importance of your birth name and date and how to use them to develop harmonics, receive memories, and reveal your divine purpose!

$16.95 • Softcover • 256 PP. • 978-1-62233-017-1

Permission to Ascend

The Great One allowed all things to be. Then there became these supplications for a greater knowledge in the physical world with the questioning, "There has to be more than this? There *has* to be more than this?" Many have asked that and said that and searched for that for years, thousands and thousands of years. The request for this further information of "there's more than this," that request has been answered, yes. And you are in the process of it.

In *Permission to Ascend*, you become aware of the humility within the self to understand the process that you call ascension. Humility is a requirement in order to get the permission that you need in order to work through this realm. This humility allows your divine force to enter you so that it can descend, and you are the humble carrier of that energy.

$16.95 • Softcover • 144 PP. • 978-1-62233-039-3

All Our Books Are Also Available as eBooks on Amazon, Apple iTunes, Google Play, and Barnes & Noble.